OPERATION
TONGA

OPERATION TONGA

THE GLIDER ASSAULT: 6 JUNE 1944

KEVIN SHANNON
AND
STEPHEN WRIGHT

FONTHILL

Learn more about Fonthill Media. Join our mailing list to find out about our latest titles and special offers at:
www.fonthillmedia.com

Fonthill Media Limited
Fonthill Media LLC
www.fonthillmedia.com
office@fonthillmedia.com

First published in the United Kingdom and the United States of America 2014

British Library Cataloguing in Publication Data:
A catalogue record for this book is available from the British Library

ISBN 978-1-78155-249-0

Typeset in 10.5pt on 13pt Sabon LT Std
Printed and bound in England

Contents

Foreword

General Sir John Hackett GCB, CBE, DSO, MC, MA, BLITT, LLD

Of much that has come my way in a long and varied life few things have given me as much satisfaction as acceptance by the Glider Pilot Regimental Association as their Patron.

Though an enthusiast for the flying of light aircraft (I qualified on a Gypsy Moth in Heliopolis in 1935 and for some years owned Puss Moth G-ABTD which gave me many hours and much pleasure up and down the Middle East until the war; after which, at home, I flew Chipmunks and Beavers) I was never a glider pilot. I had not, in fact, known any glider pilots until I brought the 4th Parachute Brigade over from Palestine to join the First Airborne Division in Tunisia in 1943. I soon began to discover the extraordinarily high quality of this unique body of men. These were total soldiers, expert airmen and at the same time splendidly effective fighting men in the land battle.

No one below the rank of sergeant was an acceptable candidate for transfer to the Glider Pilot Regiment and many were officers and warrant officers. When the division invaded Sicily on the night of 9/10 July 1943 my own brigade was left behind in North Africa in reserve and I was acting commander at our divisional base. The operation was a disaster. U.S. Troop Carrier Command tug pilots, flying C-47s with no crew protection and no self-sealing tanks, with virtually no military experience, were panic-stricken at their first encounter with flak and cast off their Horsa gliders over the sea at night, facing high wind, too far out for most to make a landfall. Over 300 British airborne soldiers drowned and glider pilots who were recovered from the sea came back looking for tug pilots' throats to cut. I saw no option but to confine them all to camp until after the American parade for the award of decorations for gallantry, by which time the admirable qualities always to be found in glider pilots had reasserted themselves and calm was restored. I learnt a great deal about glider pilots in those days and found much to admire. The esteem in which

I then held them was never to grow less. In the Arnhem Battle my own 4th Parachute Brigade was destroyed. Out of 2,300 men who went in only some 200 came out, but the heaviest casualties in the whole division were those of glider pilots fighting on the ground after they landed, when 229 of them were killed.

This book by Kevin Shannon and Stephen Wright is about the bold and spectacular airborne action which, code-named Operation Tonga, opened the Second Front in World War II. Many who survived the Sicilian disaster were later to survive Market Garden too.

The account given here of Operation *Tonga* is the best piece of writing about gliders in war, and the men who flew them in and then fought it out on the ground, that I have seen. It makes enthralling reading, using abundant first-hand evidence from pilots themselves about training, the preparation, planning and launching of the operation, the flight into action and the hazards of arrival and finally the adventures of pilots fortunate enough to survive it all, who then became evaders and were finally made prisoners of war. The exact and detailed documentation of Glider Pilots, which is appended to the narrative, will remain a valuable historical source.

I am confident that no other body of British fighting men can match the record of this regiment, now defunct, whose unique performance deserves the highest praise. It will never be forgotten and readers of this book will readily understand why.

Preface

In 1994, the fiftieth anniversary of the Normandy landings, we saw the publication of *One Night in June*, an account of the Glider Pilot Regiment's role in Operation *Tonga*, the first stage of the Airborne assault in the landings. This operation was vital to the success of the whole D-Day plan and included the now famous attacks on the Merville Battery and the bridges over the Orne River and the Caen Canal. The equally important, though less well known, part of the operation was to blow up the bridges over the Dives River and to provide an anti-tank screen to protect the southern and eastern flanks of the invasion beaches from counter attacks, by the 12th SS and 21st Panzer Divisions, in the early and vulnerable stages of the landings.

The part played by the Glider Pilot Regiment on the night of 5/6 June had never, in our opinion, been adequately covered in any other published volume. The contribution of the nine gliders which took part in the coup de main landings has been well documented in the many books on the Normandy landings. However, even here, there have been many factual errors. Of the other eighty-nine gliders which took part in *Tonga* little has been written. Our book was intended to set the record straight and a great deal of it was written from the viewpoint of the pilots, their passengers, the crews of their tug aircraft and those who witnessed this night-time landing.

Now, thanks to Fonthill Media, we have been given the opportunity to have an updated edition published in the seventieth anniversary year. In the intervening years between the two editions, new documents containing first-hand accounts have been released into the public domain allowing us to add more detail to the fate of individual gliders and their pilots and passengers.

We dedicate the book to two *Tonga* pilots in particular—Billy Marfleet and Bill Shannon—whose experiences prompted the writing of this book, and to all those who served in the Glider Pilot Regiment.

Acknowledgments

We would like to acknowledge the help of the following organisations and people for the part they played in the writing of this book.

'Andy' Andrews, Robert Ashby, Fred Baacke, Diana Bailey (née Chadwick), Arnold Baldwin, Geoff Barkway, Ron Bartley, Johnny Bowen, *Brighton Evening Argus*, David Brook, George Brownlee, Fred Corry, Bob Cross, John Cross, D-Day Aviation Museum, Appuldram, Chris Dodwell, Sandy Dow, Denis Edwards, J. Edwards, Taff Evans, Robert Falkingham, Ralph Fellows, Glider Pilot Regimental Association, General Sir John Hackett, David Hall, Ron Hellyer, Bryan Helme, Roy Howard, Mme Lydie Herbé, Henry Humberstone, Ken Kirkham, Tony Leake, Geoffrey Lockwood, Macdonald & Co., for permission to quote from George Chatterton's The Wings of Pegasus, M. Robert Marie, William Meiklejohn, Hugo Mitchell, Iain Murray, Museum of Army Flying, Chris Musitano (for giving permission to use his late father's story), George Nye, Frank Ockenden, Terence Otway, Aubrey Pickwoad, Hugh Pond, John Porter, John Potts, Eddie Raspison, Alan Richards, Tim Roseveare, Paddy Senier, John Shave, Bill Shannon, Jock Simpson, Ernie Stocker, Mike Strong; M. Guy Tabary, Ian Toler, Vin Tyndall, Mme. Jeanne Vallois; Laurie Weeden, Eric Wilson, Philip Wilson, Don Wood, John Woodhouse (for the German translation). In particular we must acknowledge the great help and encouragement received from 'Andy' Andrews, David Hall, Laurie Weeden and Tony Leake.

Chapter One

Horsa glider *PF 715* wallowed like a ponderous great whale on the end of the hempen rope. Staff Sergeant 'Taffy' Howe and his second pilot, Sergeant Bill Shannon, fought the craft's tendency to roll with extra pressure on the rudder pedals. At the best of times a laden Horsa needed much physical effort to fly, but tonight the two young pilots had flown the whole trip with full left rudder applied, an effort that on any other occasion would have exhausted them. Tonight was different. The months of blood, sweat and practice belonged to the past. This was it, the Second Front, and they and their comrades were spearheading it.

In the darkness ahead, and slightly above them, they could make out the silhouette of the Halifax V skippered by Flight Sergeant Cuncliffe, an Australian from 298 Squadron. Taffy kept his eyes on the dull red glows of the exhaust stubs protruding from the Halifax's four engines, their best aid to keeping station on the tug. Meanwhile Bill monitored their few instruments and kept a watch for other aircraft, the muted growl washing back from the engines just loud enough to prevent casual conversation.

'Horsa on the port beam, Taffy,' Bill informed the first pilot.

'Can you see who it is, Bill?'

An exchange of signals soon established that the other glider was Chalk 125 [so called because the numbers were written on the fuselage in chalk], crewed by Staff Sergeant George Phillpott and Sergeant Eric 'Snip' Taylor. The latter was a close friend of Bill Shannon and the two drinking buddies swapped rude greetings in Morse by torchlight. As the two gliders and tug combinations headed towards the French coast at a height of 1,200 feet, the scattered cloud began to get thicker. Taffy was concentrating hard on keeping in the correct low-tow position, sweat from the effort running down his face. Sometimes they lost all sight of the tug, relying solely on the Tow Angle Indicator, the so-called 'Angle of Dangle', to tell them where they were in relation to the Halifax.

Through the patchy cloud Bill made out a darker line ahead. The approach to the French Coast brought the dangers of flak. As shells started to burst around them there was a blinding flash from port. Frozen on Bill's retina was a sight he was to remember for the next forty-five years as the neighbouring Horsa glider blew apart in mid-air, a direct hit on its trailer load of anti-tank mines. The remains of the glider, its two pilots, seven troops, jeep, trailer and motorcycle tumbled towards the dark sea below. Bill turned to Taffy and shook his head sadly.

No words were necessary, or indeed possible, as their own tug pilot took the destruction of the other glider as a signal to begin a series of violent evasive manoeuvres of his own. Vainly, they tried to follow the wildly corkscrewing Halifax in and out of cloud, until the inevitable happened and the tow-rope broke, or was released. With a crash it fell back on the canopy, breaking the two panels above Bill's head. At intervals Bill called out the altimeter readings to Taffy, both pilots having hands on the controls just in case. They had been released at 1,400 feet. A Horsa sank at a rate of over 400 feet a minute when laden. *PF 715* wasn't so much laden as overloaded!

At 800 feet they broke clear of the cloud and found that they were directly over the shore line. Beneath them were roofs and church spires, while ahead, all they could see was a vast sheet of water where the Germans had flooded the land. No suitable landing site was to be seen as flak continually struck the frail plywood and canvas of the Horsa.

* * * * *

The Second Front had been on the minds of politicians, soldiers, and their worried families for some time now. Stalin, in beleaguered Russia, had demanded it from Roosevelt and Churchill. In occupied Europe millions suffered under the Nazi heel. After Sicily came Italy, the so-called 'soft underbelly of Europe'. For some, the Second Front had already started.

Members of the Eighth Army, struggling their way slowly northwards through the mud of Italy, facing, time after time, mountain defences and opposed river crossings, were certain that it had. However, it was clear that if Hitler was to be defeated and Europe freed from tyranny, then the best invasion route was through France.

Hitler, himself, was as aware of this as the Allies and he had given the task of defending the French coast to his most able general, *Feldmarschall* Erwin Rommel. As the months of 1944 ticked by, the defences on the coast became more and more daunting. The Germans were the pioneers of airborne invasion in the Low Countries and Crete and were well aware of the danger posed by parachutists and glider-borne troops. The defences of France were layered inland to combat this threat.

On the beaches, batteries of artillery and mines by the million, backed up by steel obstacles, denied the Allies easy access and provided the armoured carapace for Fortress Europe. Inland, Rommel was in the process of obstructing all viable landing fields with wooden poles. The Pas de Calais was thought by Hitler to be the most likely landing area, being the closest to Britain and having major ports. This delusion was encouraged by Allied intelligence with numerous subtle ploys. The result of this thinking was the deployment of Germany's best forces in positions to deal with invasion from this direction. This wasn't to say that the Normandy area was undefended, far from it. Army Group B, under the command of Rommel, covered the area from St Nazaire, up the Channel and along the North Sea coast of Europe into the Netherlands. The Seventh Army, commanded by *Generaloberst* Friedrich Dollman, had the sector from St Nazaire to just east of Caen, while the Fifteenth Army under *Generaloberst* Hans Von Salmuth controlled most of the Channel coast. Because of the belief that the Pas de Calais was the most likely invasion area the Fifteenth Army received priority in both weapons and men.

The Seventh Army had three under-strength infantry divisions facing the invasion beaches. In the American sector were the 709 Coastal Defence and 352 Field Divisions, while the 716 Infantry Division was deployed behind the beaches allocated to the British. All of these infantry units relied heavily on Eastern European conscripts from Poland and the Ukraine as well as men deemed medically unfit for the Eastern Front. The only armour the Seventh Army possessed was the 21st Panzer Division, which was only partially equipped with the Panther, most of its armour being an earlier tank, the PkW IV or the StGW III, an assault gun. 21st Panzer had been a first-class unit, but had been mauled in North Africa in 1942 and then destroyed in Tunisia in May 1943. Reformed in the summer of 1943, it had remained in France since then, the vast majority of its personnel inexperienced in combat.

While the Fifteenth Army was better off than its counterpart, the Seventh, it still had shortages of both men and equipment. The 711 Infantry Division in the Orne and Dives area had an equally high percentage of second-rate troops and equipment. To the south and east was the 12th SS Panzer Division, *Hitler Jugend*, a highly trained, well-motivated, but untried unit. The terrain in Normandy favoured the defenders. The *bocage*, a countryside of high, strong hedgerows, small fields and sunken lanes, was a tank commander's nightmare. Every hedge could conceal an infantryman with an anti-tank weapon or a self-propelled gun. The Germans had a considerable technological lead over the British when it came to man portable anti-tank weapons, with the *panzerfaust* and *panzerschreck* rocket launchers, both of which fired a HEAT (High Explosive Anti-tank) projectile. The British PIAT (Projector Infantry

Anti-tank), a spring-powered Heath Robinson affair, could be effective at point-blank range, provided you did not want to fire downwards, as the missile would just slide out of the end of the barrel. To further exacerbate tactical considerations, the strong spring made cocking the weapon a Herculean task, only possible in the prone position with extreme difficulty. The warhead would not penetrate the frontal armour of the largest of the German tanks and some infantrymen had had the disconcerting experience of scoring a direct hit on a tank, with the explosion blowing all the hatches open, only to see, a second later, an arm reach up out of the turret, shut the hatch and then the tank continue fighting.

The Germans also had excellent field artillery, both in conventional guns and rocket launchers, their tactics tried and proven on the Eastern front. Axis infantry units were also skilled in the use of mortar fire and, as defenders, they would have more supplies of ammunition than the lightly-equipped airborne troops that would oppose them. Until dawn, the Allies would have to rely mainly on the light mortars that the attacking infantry were issued with and the small amounts of ammunition that could be carried. The trump card that the Allies would play in the initial phases of the Invasion would be the devastating firepower from ships of all size that could be called down on target by teams of highly-trained observers, who had landed by parachute and in gliders. The Allies were confident that the surprise and confusion caused by massed landings from the air would not allow the Germans to deploy their artillery effectively until daylight. By then Allied airpower and naval gunfire could be used to full effect.

The decisive factor therefore in the early stages of the invasion, before Allied air superiority could be brought into play, would be the spirit, training and aggression of the troops, an area in which General Gale was confident that his troops had overwhelming superiority.

The planners of Operation *Overlord* had one overriding concern. The troops landing must be allowed to establish a strong beach-head so that Allied strength could be built up for the push inland and not trapped in the immediate beach area. Churchill, who had played such a major part in the fiasco at Gallipoli in World War I, had nightmares about the Channel running red with British blood and didn't want a repeat of either that or the slaughter on the beach at Dieppe. Intelligence sources knew the strength and dispositions of German forces in the Normandy area and the planners were fully aware of the need to prevent 21st Panzer from getting to the beach-head in the early stages of the landing. They were also more than aware that the high ground to the east of the River Orne gave direct observation of the beach-head area. If this ground was left in the hands of the enemy, then accurate artillery fire could be brought to bear on the landings. The only way to deny the Germans the use of this terrain in the initial stages of the assault was to seize the area prior to the main invasion. This meant an airborne assault. *Neptune Operational Order No. 1* (WO 171/1283 174049) to the Officer Commanding No. 1 Wing, Glider Pilot Regiment lists the tasks of 6th Airborne Division.

6 AIRBORNE DIVISION with 1SS BDE under command will protect the LEFT flank of 1 Corps, by denying the enemy the use of the area between the Rs. ORNE and DIVES, NORTH of the rd. TROARN 1667—SANNERVILLE 1367 COLOMBELLES 0770. 6 Airborne Div will also attack and delay enemy reserves and reinforcements attempting to move towards CAEN from the EAST and S.E.

5 Para Bde Group will land night D-1/D-Day in area NORTH of RANVILLE and operate in area of BENOUVILLE—RANVILLE.

(a) Tasks

(i) Seize the crossings over the R.ORNE and CANAL DE CAEN at BENOUVILLE 098748 and RANVILLE 1173.

(ii) Secure and hold area BENOUVILLE 0970—RANVILLE 1173—LE BAS DE RANVILLE 105735.

(iii) Capture the Bty at 107765.

(iv) Clear and protect LZ 'N' by P-2 hrs (D-1 Day) and Z hr. (D-Day).

3 Para Bde Group will land night D-1 / D-Day on L.Z. & D .Z. V and K, and operate in area TROARN 177680, VARAVILLE-Bty 154776.

(a) Tasks

(i) Demolish the bridges at TROARN 1667—ROBEHOMME 1872— VARAVILLE 1875 by H hour plus 2 hrs.

(ii) Hold the above area until relieved by 1 SS Bde.'

Operation *Neptune*, the initial phase of the invasion of Normandy (Operation Overlord) included the airborne assault on Normandy which was split into three sections: *Tonga*, involving ninety-eight gliders, would precede the seaborne landings to carry out the tasks of 5th and 3rd Parachute Brigade Groups between midnight and 0400 hours on the morning of D-Day; *Mallard*, involving two hundred and fifty-six gliders, was to be the main airborne landing of heavy equipment, especially more seventeen-pounder anti-tank guns and glider-borne troops and due to land round 9 p.m. in the evening of D-Day; *Rob-Roy* was to be a later resupply operation.

It was not planned to deliver the main force for *Tonga* by glider as not only was this deemed far too risky, but there was a shortage of suitable tug aircraft and trained aircrews. Less training was needed for pilots who were to be used to drop parachutists, so the limited resources were concentrated in this area. Allied air commanders, including Air Chief Marshal Sir

Trafford Leigh-Mallory, were of the opinion that up to fifty per cent casualties from flak would have been the order of the day. (Happily, this estimate was proved to be extremely pessimistic.)

A key element to *Tonga* was the accurate placement of the parachutists. Should the sticks, as an aircraft load was known, be widely scattered then vital hours would be wasted. At best, the element of surprise would be lost, and at worst, the airborne troops mopped up piecemeal by the Germans. If the gliders were unable to find their targets then a similar result would have occurred. Therefore accurate navigation by the RAF was essential, as was the marking of the DZs and LZs. 'Gee', a radio navigation beam, was fitted to many of the tugs and transports. Aircraft were also fitted with 'Rebecca', a receiver which homed in on a signal from a ground based transmitter, 'Eureka'. The zones would also be marked with Holophane lights in the shape of a letter 'T', only visible to pilots approaching into wind, and beacons flashing a Morse letter. These and Eureka beacons would be placed by pathfinders of 22nd Independent Parachute Company shortly before the landings.

'Unique' is a descriptive word that is frequently misused by people who mean rare or special. The Glider Pilot Regiment was special, but it was also unique. The Germans and Americans, who both used gliders to carry their troops into action, did not have pilots trained to the same degree. After the American glider pilot had landed his charges he left for the rear areas, his job done.

The British glider pilot was different. Once he had landed he discarded his pilot's goggles and picked up his rifle. To become a member of the Glider Pilot Regiment a recruit had not only to satisfy the RAF aircrew education and aptitude requirements but also to be able to function as an airborne soldier alongside troops famed for their aggressive fighting spirit. A man capable of this was a very special soldier indeed. The lowest rank held by a trained member of the regiment was sergeant and every first pilot was a staff sergeant at the very least. The *esprit de corps* and fighting spirit of the men in the regiment was second to none. That was why they were there. They were, as Colonel Chatterton once called them, 'Total Soldiers'.

Formed in 1942, the Regiment had already been blooded. Operation *Freshman*, a small raid on a heavy water plant in Norway in November 1942, had been a disaster due to adverse weather conditions. One tug and glider combination flew into a mountain, and the other glider crashed after the tow rope broke due to heavy icing, the survivors were then murdered in a Gestapo cell.

Only the heavy equipment for 3rd Parachute Brigade Group was to land by glider. Six gliders of 'F' Squadron, the Glider Pilot Regiment would take off from Blakehill Farm loaded with jeeps, explosives and No. 2 Section,

224 Parachute Field Ambulance, bound for LZ 'K'. 8th Parachute Battalion would use these to blow the River Dives bridges. Seven gliders of 'E' Squadron would take off from Down Ampney and would land on LZ 'V' in support of the 3rd Parachute Brigade operation. From Harwell, four gliders of' 'A' Squadron, carrying elements of the 9th Parachute Battalion and No. 3 Section 224 Parachute Field Ambulance would also land on LZ 'V'.

The first gliders to take off would be six Horsas under the command of 'B' Squadron from Tarrant Rushton. These crews had been detached in May from their parent squadrons to train for a 'special operation'. These gliders, carrying troops of 'D' and 'B' Companies, the 2nd Oxfordshire and Buckinghamshire Light Infantry, were to take the two bridges over the River Orne and the Caen Canal and hold them until relieved by elements of 1st Special Service Brigade which was landing by sea. This operation, known as *Coup de Main*, appeared, on paper at least, to be the hardest of all the tasks for the Glider Pilot Regiment that night. Six gliders had to find two very small LZs without the benefit of lights or radio navigation beacons, and disgorge their troops intact, close enough to the bridges to prevent the Germans setting off prepared demolition charges, but not so close that they hit obstacles and injured the troops inside the fragile craft. There would be no second chance. The pilots of the Horsas had to get the landing approach right first time!

9th Parachute Battalion, under the command of Lieutenant-Colonel Terence Otway DSO, had been given the task of taking and destroying the Merville Battery, thought to contain large calibre guns and sited in a position to threaten the whole left flank of Sword Beach. It was planned to land three gliders of 'B' Squadron, containing sixty-three men of 'A' Company 9th Parachute Battalion and 591 Parachute Squadron, R.E. in another *coup de main* operation directly on the battery during the night attack, but most of the six hundred men from the 9th Battalion would be dropped by parachute onto DZ 'V' earlier.

Seven gliders from 'E' Squadron were to take-off from Down Ampney at 2250 hours on 5 June and land on LZ 'V'. These craft would carry two six-pounder anti-tank guns, jeeps and equipment for Headquarters 3rd Parachute Brigade and the 1st (Canadian) Parachute Battalion. Also included would be two ambulance jeeps. 'A' Squadron at Harwell would also send four gliders to LZ 'V'. Three of these would carry heavy equipment vital to Otway's plan to seize the Merville Battery, including light bridging sections to cross the anti-tank ditch. The fourth glider was to take a jeep and trailer of No. 3 Section, 224 Parachute Field Ambulance.

Staff Sergeant William Meiklejohn, who landed in Normandy on the evening of 6 June on Operation Mallard, described the selection process of these four Squadron crews:

I can well remember the competition to select these crews. A spot was placed on the runway and a small sum of money was offered to those who touched down nearest to the mark. The first four crews were in due course detailed for the night landing. I must have been very naive for it wasn't till long after that I realised what the competition was all about. You must admit from an officers' point of view it was a good way to pick crews who had to do a spot landing. Tonga was very hush-hush and no-one spoke about it at all. The crews were away from the barrack room quite a lot—we assumed that they were being briefed.

Later that night a further sixty-eight Horsas and four Hamilcars would take off for France. From Brize Norton, 'B' Squadron would send seventeen Horsas laden with equipment for 5th Parachute Brigade and the Royal Engineers to LZ 'N'. 'A' Squadron at Harwell was to contribute a further twenty-one Horsas for LZ 'N' carrying 6th Airborne's Headquarters. Squadron CO, Major S. C. 'Billy' Griffith, DFC, the test cricketer, and Squadron Sergeant-Major Ken Mew in Chalk 70 had the task of carrying the commander of 6th Airborne, Major-General Richard 'Windy' Gale, a larger-than-life character. From Tarrant Rushton, 'D' Squadron, under Major J. P. 'Daddy' Lyne, was tasked to send thirty Horsas to LZ 'N', many carrying six-pounder anti-tank guns of 4th Airlanding Anti-Tank Battery. 'C' Squadron's giant Hamilcars would each carry a seventeen-pounder anti-tank gun, the only Allied anti-tank gun that could seriously inconvenience a Tiger tank. All these guns would play a vital role in the defence of the 6th Airborne area in the early stages of Overlord.

The worry about the Tiger was overestimated in Normandy. Luckily for the Allies the Germans actually had very few. 21st Panzer was only partially equipped with the Panther, most of their troops were still using the PKW IV, which was vulnerable to the six-pounder. The decision of the commander of 21st Panzer to hold back the Panthers in his initial engagements with 6th Airborne was probably quite fortuitous for the Allies.

Chapter Two

In the early months of 1944 the build-up of troops for the invasion of Europe got underway. The wartime flying of a glider was a dangerous job in broad daylight, but in darkness with a load it was treacherous. The requirements of *Overlord* required the pilots to be expert in night flights and landings. The only way to gain expertise was constant practice. One hundred and thirty-two members of the Glider Pilot Regiment died accidentally during the three years of war. In the months leading up to D-Day the training became more realistic.

In spring 1944 the exercises began to have code names, such as *Sailor* on 3 March, *Bizz* 2 on 25 March, and on 4 April, *Dreme*. The log book of a 'D' Squadron first pilot, Staff Sergeant Sandy Dow, who had as his second pilot the Squadron OC, Major Lyne, remembers that night all too clearly:

Despite a reasonable Met. forecast on take-off, really bad weather set in somewhere over Hampshire in low, cloudy, hilly country. The Stirling tug craft was obviously having a rough time as we tried to keep in alignment. The Angle of Dangle instrument showing at one point our glider much higher than the Stirling and almost beginning to pull the powered craft's tail upwards with it. The tug pilot suggested he cast off and this manoeuvre was easily achieved by simply pulling a large red knob, automatically releasing the ball at the end of the tow-rope from its socket on the glider end. We were then in free flight and, of course, the plane much more manoeuvrable. Descending below cloud level, by direct visibility I was suddenly aware of tiny hills, knolls and trees. Initially, there was no hope of a landing spot. The search for a landing spot, together with navigation, was the task of the second pilot (most of whom had still not completed their full first pilot's training). John Lyne, the cheerfully moustached Major in this role, pointed out some typical English parkland dotted rather thickly with typical English oaks, really too close together to permit a trouble-free landing. He picked an approach track between lines of oaks. The glider nosed groundwards and as late as possible the craft was put down, relatively gently. The only means I had of stopping the glider was to clip off the tips of the wings on either side against two trees. Congratulations were shouted from my thirty-odd passengers who had been asked to brace for a crash landing. It was a humbling experience for me for the entourage were all fairly top brass—brigadiers, colonels etc., all of whom had joined the exercise as observers to accustom themselves to glider transport. For the most part, they only suffered from a general shaking up. Major Lyne and I came off worse. He suffered from surface bruises as a branch had thrust its way through the cockpit Perspex, and I was similarly scraped and had a black eye. What was more, the estate on which we had landed somewhere near Peters field in Hampshire, was known to some of the field officers aboard and the whole company was safely regaled in the big house from which communications were established with base and the outer world.

Not everyone escaped so lightly. Sergeant Bill Shannon, of 'D' Squadron, noted in his log that Horsa *LH 505*, in which he was flying as second pilot to Staff Sergeant Taffy Howe, also force landed into trees near Petersfield. He wrote shortly afterwards that '…three passengers were cut and bruised and the wheels of the jeep were buckled. Aircraft 'CAT. E'.' The laconic remark, 'CAT. E' described a glider that was fit for scrap—the fate of many a Horsa in the days leading up to Overlord.

Of the thirty Horsas from 'D' Squadron that took part in *Dreme*, twenty-two of the twenty-three that force landed crashed, with thirty-four fatalities. Staff Sergeant Bill Musitano spoke about this exercise:

When we were confined to camp we spent much time gambling, and I might well have achieved the reputation of not being a man to owe money to. Two men before and one on D-Day, died owing me small amounts. 'Dreme' was a mass landing at dusk on the grass between the runways at Brize Norton after more than three hours tow around a triangular course starting from Keevil. I was flying Horsa LH 461 with Sergeant Paddy Perry, a youngster from Southern Ireland, as second pilot. On the way we ran into low cloud and the pilot of the Stirling towing us asked us down the telephone cable if we wanted to go over or under. It is not easy to keep station in cloud so I opted for over where I could be sure of seeing his tail.
Apparently Staff Sergeant Solly Joel in another combination elected to stay under, or perhaps his tug pilot didn't give him the option. The Stirling, with six crew, the two glider pilots and twenty-six soldiers they were carrying slammed into a low hill at about one hundred and forty

miles an hour. It was said that the largest human remains were in their boots. Solly owed me £4 or £5. My second pilot, Sergeant Perry was killed on D-Day, although I didn't know this until four months later. I believe he owed me £2.

All of the fatalities on *Dreme* were in this combination of tug and glider. Few other exercises cost so much in human life for the simple reason that the 'powers-that-be' viewed the lives of trained soldiers as too valuable to risk in gliders unless strictly necessary. For most of the time concrete or steel ballast made up the weight. In Bill Shannon's scrapbook is a thin piece of plywood labelled 'Horsa LG 851. Crashed near Marnhull, Dorset. 20-3-44. Tow rope broke under strain in rough weather. Wing hit tree on approach and broke off. Aircraft spun-in from 30 feet. Load and passengers undamaged. Aircraft Cat.E.' This was *Bizz 1*.

Sandy Dow remembers more problems with the weather on *Dingo 2* on 7 May 1944. This time he had as his second pilot Squadron Sergeant Major Jack Oliver. The exercise was a mass take-off and landing on a huge illuminated 'T'. The orientation of the 'T' showed the pilots the wind direction. This detail was important as a downwind landing in a laden Horsa was hazardous bordering on the suicidal. Unfortunately for the crews, the wind veered to the opposite direction from that given at briefing.

Approximately one hundred and fifty pairs of gliders and tugs took off at two minute intervals for the landing zone. Sandy Dow's tug pilot realised that the wind had changed direction and approached the release point in the correct upwind approach. His glider, one of the first to arrive, landed safely and the crew cleared the landing zone without mishap.

Later arrivals landed in all directions. Some approached upwind, whilst others obeyed the 'T', tugs and gliders narrowly missing each other in the crowded skies. Although there were no fatalities, there was considerable damage as gliders collided with each other and obstructions on the ground.

The next weeks saw further mass exercises, both night and day, most of which proceeded with increasing smoothness and accuracy. In all, nineteen massed landings of not less than a hundred gliders were made in the build-up to D-Day. Staff Sergeant John Potts, who had been absent from flying for a number of months due to his being attached to the depot as a drill instructor, was teamed up with his friend Staff Sergeant Bill Jones of 'B' Squadron:

We were one of three aircraft dispatched to Thruxton Aerodrome where we started experimenting with night flying in daytime. This is performed by one pilot in turn wearing exceedingly blacked-out goggles and on the aerodrome they started off with a dozen or so sodium flares, the goggles only permitting you to see those flares. As the trips went by they reduced the number of flares until finally we got to three. We were given a hint that we should be landing in darkness and furthermore, whatever task we should be given, we would be in small groups.

The crews who had been selected to seize the bridges over the Orne River and Caen Canal, were undergoing intensive training of a different nature. Not for them were the massed night-time landings. Their need was pinpoint accuracy.

Sixteen pilots were chosen to go to Tarrant Rushton for specialised training. Although the operation only called for twelve, the planners were taking no chances and had allowed four extra in reserve in case of accidents. The glider crews were towed by the same RAF crew on each exercise and before too long a rapport grew between them. Colonel George Chatterton had to prove to both General Browning, commanding Airborne Forces, and General Gale that the landing was feasible. In a demonstration at Netheravon six gliders were released at a height of six thousand feet, five miles away. They landed within feet of each other in a triangle only one hundred yards from base to apex, much to the outwardly confident Chatterton's secret relief.

Training was made the responsibility of Flight Lieutenant Tom Grant, DSO, an experienced RAF tug pilot. Grant, who codenamed the training *Deadstick*, had the crews practising complicated approaches into small landing zones using stopwatches and compass. This was hard enough in daylight, but in darkness, it bordered on the impossible, yet by mid-May the crews could accomplish this in all weathers and at night, with just moonlight for guidance.

Not every exercise went smoothly. One night exercise, in front of an assembled group of top-brass, resulted in three of the six gliders being written off. One overshot the LZ and crashed and the fourth glider landed on top of the third, reducing both to scrap. For ballast each glider had been carrying a 5,000 lb steel spar from a Bailey bridge. Despite this mishap the only casualty was a sprained ankle. After forty-three such training flights they were deemed ready. For what, the crews weren't sure, until just a few days before D-Day.

During the weekend before D-Day the gliders were fitted with arrestor parachutes. Staff Sergeant Geoff Barkway, the first pilot of Chalk 93 remembers....'we never actually practised with them.' Not unnaturally the pilots were reluctant to deploy them on the actual landing.

Receiving equally specialised training were the crews selected for the landing on the Merville Battery. This phase of *Tonga* does not appear to have been given a separate code-name, official reports merely refer to the *Battery* mission of *Tonga*. These glider crews trained hard at making pinpoint landings on a marked spot and stopping as quickly as possible, within a triangle 150 yards wide by 160 yards long. To help them these gliders had also been fitted with arrestor parachutes. This group of pilots however had the opportunity to train with them. It was not just the glider pilots themselves who were on unfamiliar ground. Lieutenant Hugh Pond, a platoon commander from 'A' Coy, 9th Parachute Battalion, recalls getting the news about the forthcoming role for his platoon on D-Day:

It was a great shock for all of us in the company to be told by Lieutenant-Colonel Martin Lindsay, who was then officer commanding the 9th Battalion, that he wanted volunteers for a hazardous operation which involved going into battle by glider. He realised our disappointment as we had trained so hard on parachuting manoeuvres. Despite this the whole company stepped forward, as expected. (Who could have dared to refuse!) It was then a question of choosing the three-groups who would travel in the gliders. Married men were automatically excluded. How the final list was chosen I do not know. Presumably Major Allen Parry and the CO made the final selection. Very shortly after this we were taken to a small aerodrome and made our first acquaintance with the gliders and the glider pilots. We were horrified at the three-ply wooden structure and considered it more a joke, a toy, than a vehicle for going to war in. However, we were soon given a joy-ride and that was quite an experience. We'd had no information at all about gliders and, with parachute snobbery, tended to look down our noses at glider-borne troops. We rapidly changed our minds when we saw them going into action.

We climbed into the 'matchbox' and belted up. There were twenty-eight of us in all and we had a good laugh when we were introduced to the funnel which was the urinal. It doesn't take much to make a bunch of nervous parachutists laugh! We were most impressed by the smoothness of take-off and how Staff Sergeant Kerr, the glider pilot, manoeuvred the glider into high or low tow as required. The roar of the tug engines at full throttle gave us the impression of normal aircraft flight but, after cast-off, the silence was most impressive and almost eerie with the wind sighing through the wing struts and other projections. The landing on the grass strip was very smooth and we all considered that whatever the 'hazardous' operation was it would be a piece of cake!

The rest of the Battalion subjected us to a lot of good-hearted sarcasm. They thought we'd landed an easy number! For the next few weeks S/Sgt Kerr rehearsed, with us on board, trying to land in a white circle, drawn by a man using a sports ground lining machine. The circle seemed quite tiny but Kerr became an expert. Eventually the secrecy wraps were taken off the operation and all but the name of the battery to be attacked was revealed. It was somewhat of a shock to learn that the glider would probably land and break off its wings on the gun emplacements. We were assured that the glider was designed and constructed that way.

When it came to live ammunition exercises we were told that we couldn't wreck a glider just for practice so we were marched into the centre of the mock-up battery and stood there, feeling rather silly, waiting for our comrades to arrive, and as one bright spark put it—waiting to be shot by our own people! After this it was considered important that we should have some means of easy identification. We had passwords (something stupid like Pee-Off and Olly-Olly) and there was also a patch either on our backs or arms. Captain Gordon-Brown, an architect, leader of the glider party, decided that we would all wear a luminous painted skull and crossbones on our right breast. A little bit of bravado and subsequent embarrassment.

It was not only the glider pilots who were busy preparing for the operation. Lieutenant Ralph Fellows, the map reader in a 271 Squadron Dakota flown by Major P. S. Joubert, a former World War I fighter pilot from South Africa, remembers spending their days practising towing gliders and dropping parachutists and supply panniers by day and night:

On 22 April a few crews, including ours, dropped leaflets over France. I guess it was to give us experience of a flight to the Normandy coast and inland. At that time we had no idea that we would see it again so shortly.

The tug crews and glider pilots formed a very close relationship during this period, messing together and whenever possible teaming up for training flights. At their respective bases, the squadrons of the Glider Pilot Regiment were selecting and training the crews for *Tonga*. By mid-May, Flight Lieutenant Aubrey Pickwoad, OC of 14 Flight, 'F' Squadron had selected six crews for the landing on LZ 'K' on the basis of their performance on night landing exercises.

It should be remembered that no-one had ever made a massed night assault by glider before, the landing in Sicily being on a much smaller scale. The Glider Pilot Regiment was pioneering the technique, and in many quarters there was a feeling that the operations were doomed to failure. Not all their training was involved with landing. The pilots were also soldiers and as such had other skills to hone.

A soldier has to be able to fight. The pilots' rigorous routine included plenty of exercise. They took part in battle training with small arms and explosives and the pilots whose gliders were to carry six-pounder anti-tank guns were trained gunners.

Sergeant Bill Shannon had this to say about training in street warfare with Otway's 9th Parachute Battalion:

We were acting as enemy for the Paras in a blitzed part of London. It was very realistic training and we were allowed to use explosives to 'mousehole' through house walls in a row of terraces. I remember I wasn't at all well one day, having a dose of 'flu. I must have passed out and when I woke up, they'd all buggered off and left me behind! I had to walk across London to the barracks where we were staying. It wasn't so much the walk, it was the fact that I was wearing German uniform and carrying a Schmeisser. Not one person challenged me, the whole way. In fact I lost count of the number of times I was saluted!'

In these days of computer games we tend to be blasé about audio-visual presentations. The pilots in the days leading up to D-Day were treated to the best that the motion picture industry could give them. A fast-flying photo-reconnaissance Mosquito had flown the exact routes that the gliders would be taking in daylight. A model had been constructed and a film made with a camera run over it slowly, and the routes and main landmarks shown on maps. The back-room boys had processed this film in such a way that it simulated the glider pilot's eye view at night under several different lighting conditions. Once they were confined to barracks in the days leading up to Overlord the pilots were able to go to the briefing room and view this film as many times as they liked. The model makers had also excelled themselves and scale models of all the targets were available. These were constantly altered as new reconnaissance photographs became available.

There was initially great concern that the operations had been compromised when photographs showing post holes on the LZs appeared, but it was soon realised that this outbreak of *Rommelspargen* (Rommel's Asparagus) was not just confined to the invasion area. Within hours of the arrival of these photographs the models had been updated. The presence of poles on the LZs wasn't the problem that some thought it was, as many of the pilots saw them as a way of bringing the gliders to a quicker halt. They planned to aim the nose between two poles and use the fragile wings as brakes! Nonetheless, the planners had allocated parachute engineers for the early drops to clear a path for the first of the gliders.

The exercise that all the pilots had to be familiar with was unloading the gliders. The Horsa Mk.I was loaded by manoeuvring the jeep, trailer or gun up a ramp and then manhandling it around ninety degrees through the side door and into the fuselage. This process was heavy physical work, hard on the knuckles and other vulnerable parts of the soft human frame, and very time consuming. It was equally difficult to unload the same way and totally impractical in a tactical situation, so the designers had come up with a solution allowing the whole tail section of the glider to be unbolted just aft of the main span. In theory, the relatively 'quick-release' bolts could be undone by the pilots in a matter of minutes and the tail would just fall away, a ramp carried inside the Horsa attached and the jeep driven out.

In practice things didn't usually work out so easily. The idea of two men calmly wielding a spanner in total darkness, whilst under fire, and sheltered by nothing more substantial than plywood and canvas would have been laughable if it hadn't been the only solution. Explosive bolts had been tried and shelved as the explosions not only blew the tail off, but often damaged the load. Should the load consist of petrol, ammunition or explosives, which most did, then this was clearly out of the question! On the many training exercises there had been little trouble with tail bolts. This was because most of the landings had been on clear, level LZs and also on most of the exercises, the load was only ballast and therefore there had been no need to take the tail off. After the glider had cannoned off trees, other gliders and through hedges and fences the airframe wasn't always as straight as it had been when it had left the makers! Frequently, the glider was also canted at an impossible angle due to part of the undercarriage having been ripped off against some obstruction, a combination of circumstances that was to cause some crews untold sweat, labour and heartache on the actual operation.

The problem was later recognised by the manufacturers who solved it with the Horsa Mk.II. In this craft, the entire nose section swung to one side on hinges fitted to the starboard side. The entire process was brought about by just two levers on the port side of the forward bulkhead of the main cabin, which had locking pins fitted to prevent inadvertent use in flight. Not only did this make unloading easier, but it also simplified loading. Sadly, no Mk.II's flew on *Tonga*.

'B' Squadron's Account of Operation Neptune (WO171/1283 174049) states that on '25th May preliminary briefing took place at Wing HQ of the officers concerned in the various operations. Maps and photographs were studied and certain details of intelligence summaries were given.' From that date those who had been briefed were confined to camp. On 2 June preliminary briefing of Captain Smellie's crews (those going on *Tonga*) took place at the station and on the 3rd a more detailed picture of their part of the operation was outlined. In the evening of that day the tug and glider crews concerned had a get together to discuss any matters regarding the operations. On Sunday there was no briefing whatsoever and still no indication of when the operation would take place.

On the 5th the crews were given their final briefings. Now, not only did they know where and how, they also knew when.

Chapter Three

The 5th of June was a tense day for many young men. All over the south of England the mechanical task of stripping, cleaning and oiling already pristine weapons was carried out again and again and kit was counted and checked. In the preceding days the crews had selected their personal weapons and zeroed them in the butts. At Tarrant Rushton, peacetime pub landlord, Staff Sergeant Bill Musitano of 'D' Squadron, older than most of the pilots, remembers the, literally staggering, choice:

> We were told to select whatever weapons and equipment we thought we might need. The choice was enormous. Bren guns, .303 Lee Enfields, .38 revolvers, shovels, compasses, daggers, ground sheets, ration packs of varying sizes, steel helmets, binoculars, flying boots (even though it was June), army boots or shoes. We made a selection, we were paraded, and started on a march. I don't think I marched more than a quarter of a mile carrying almost a hundredweight of goodies before I fell out. By this time I knew what my Horsa would be carrying, so I settled for a Bren gun, a dagger and a watch. I do not remember what I had on my head but I'm sure I had a pair of army boots on my feet. You don't need a very delicate touch to fly a Horsa. I packed the rest of the smaller items on offer into my kit-bag and left it behind. This included the revolver which I eventually sold to a gun dealer in Falmouth for £11!'

Bill Musitano's friend, Staff Sergeant Sandy Dow, known to the rest of the squadron as 'Jock', was another aircraft commander. He remembers having to sew silk maps, French currency and assorted escape kit into the lining of his smock. 'We were all in the best spirits and humour,' he said.

Sergeant Bill Shannon in a letter to a friend:

> There was a general mood of elation abroad! It was about 3 p.m. on a hot sunny afternoon that we knew D-Day had been decided and the balloon was up. We had been lying out in an adjacent field sunbathing when

we were called to flight stores. There, we were issued with detonators for grenades, morphia packs, two twenty-four hour ration packs and cigarettes. We all knew that these stores were only to be issued on D minus one. So this is it! Tomorrow, Tuesday, will be the first day of the invasion. Back at the billet we burnt letters, photographs and threw all the old junk out of our kits, so that the fireplace was cluttered up with old boxes, tins, clothing, magazines, old and surplus equipment and half-used patent medicines. We then sat down to gingerly prime our grenades. At 4 p.m. we went for the last run-through of the now familiar film and our preliminary briefing.

The priming of the Mills 36 Grenade was always a delicate task. The grenades and detonators were packed separately for obvious reasons. The letter continued:

The main briefing was at 9 p.m. in the Operations Room and took place in an atmosphere that was strained and unreal, the lamps shining down dimly through the ascending smoke on the sweating faces and mechanically chewing jaws of the tug and glider crews. We got the gen on weather, wind, heights, fighter protection and a thousand and one other details vital to the success of the operation. After this the glider pilots were briefed separately as to the disposition of the enemy on the ground. We were relieved to hear that the nearest Panzer troops were some sixteen miles away. We were to dig in on the left flank of the British Second Army and hold off the 21st Panzer Division which was known to be in that area. For this purpose we were taking over a battery of artillery and attached signals. Major John (Daddy) Lyne, our squadron commander, wished us lots of luck and promised to keep us out of as much trouble as possible, which appealed to all of us.

After briefing we walked down to the Towpath to see the first six gliders take-off to strike the first blows for the liberation of Europe. These were the 'Deadstick' boys who were to land on the bridges over the River Orne and the Caen Canal and keep the German garrison from blowing the demolition charges. It was a thrilling sight to see the six 'first' take-off and a large crowd stood on the perimeter track and watched them until they had disappeared altogether. Everyone's heart and thoughts were with them, and those of us who were next to go, thought our stomachs were there too! When there was nothing more to see or hear we wandered off to the Mess for supper. The cooks had really done us well. Bill, the fat LAC, who was the champion duff-maker, presided over his staff and they served us with egg, bacon, sausage and chips. Although the cooking was excellent, none of us felt very hungry and many left their food almost untouched. 11pm.—in another four hours we shall be in the thick of it, fighting for our lives.

The troops inside those six gliders which had just departed had been feeling no less nervous. Private Denis Edwards of 25 Platoon, 2nd Battalion, the Oxfordshire and Buckinghamshire Light Infantry, was nineteen years old and terrified:

At the airfield that day we had sat around drinking tea and cracking corny jokes. Everyone tried to seem unconcerned, but I am sure, that like me, their stomachs were churning. The gliders were already in position behind their respective towing bombers and many of the lads had exercised their artistic talents on the fuselages of the craft that were to take them to Normandy. The time dragged until at 2200 hours we clambered aboard our gliders wishing each other good luck, singing and cracking jokes.

At 2256 hours the steady hum of the bomber's engines suddenly increased to a deafening roar. My muscles tightened, a cold shiver ran up and down my spine, I went hot and cold and sang for all I was worth to stop my teeth from chattering. Suddenly there was a violent jerk and a loud twang as the slack on the thick tow-rope was taken up by the tug-plane. The glider rolled slowly forwards and my throat tightened as the plywood flying-box gathered speed and someone shouted "Ang on driver. I'm on the wrong bloody train. I thought this one was for London. Let me off!'

I experienced the most interesting psychological change during the few minutes before and after the take-off. As I climbed aboard and strapped myself into my seat I felt tight, strange and extremely nervous. I felt as if I was in some fantasy dream world and expected that at any moment I would wake up from this unreality and find that I was back in the barrack room at Bulford Camp. It was like some weird nightmare and whilst we laughed and sang to raise our spirits, and to show that we were not scared, speaking personally, I was frightened to death.

The very idea of carrying out a night-time landing of such a small force into the midst of the German army seemed to me to be little more than a suicide mission. Yet in spite of that, at the very moment that the glider finally parted company with the ground, I underwent a complete change. Whether some kindly guardian angel took my hand I do not know. The feeling of total fright immediately vanished and was replaced by sheer exhilaration. For some reason I felt very pleased with myself—on top of the world—and it was almost as though I couldn't care less. I remember thinking to myself: 'You've had it, chum. It's no good worrying any more. The die has been cast and what is to be will be and there is nothing you can do about it.

An hour later Bill Shannon and his comrades were about to follow the six gliders:

At midnight we boarded the flight truck, some twenty of us squeezing into and clinging onto a 15 cwt. We took flasks of tea and packets of sandwiches from the Mess and all the way to the runway we sang our favourite songs. Arriving at our aircraft we camouflaged ourselves, faces and hands, with black and green grease paint and dispersed to our own kites. Taffy and I were in Chalk 123, the twenty-seventh in line for take-off. Our load consisted of a motorcycle, jeep and trailer, containing anti-tank grenades, ammunition, batteries and a powerful wireless set. We had five men of the Royal Corps of Signals on board: Ginger the motorcyclist, Jock the mechanic, Peter and another Jock the wireless operators, and Bert the lance-corporal driver who was in charge of the signalmen.

Chalk 123 took off for France at 0143 hours. The twenty-four hour postponement, due to the poor weather, gave the crews an extra night in their beds. Ron Hellyer and his comrades spent the evening of the 4th in the Mess:

We were having a drink instead of heading into occupied territory. One of our number was Taffy Hughes, who was reputed to be able to tell fortunes. Someone got him to do this and, with great hilarity and ribald badinage, Taffy read our palms. I am not a great believer in mystique or the occult and it wasn't until long after that I remembered that when he got to Vic's palm, Taffy went very serious, very quiet and, muttering something about 'there's no future in this game anyway', refused to do any more palm reading.

I can't remember much about the day of June 5th. Obviously the hours flew by with loading, checking and double checking, last minute chat with Squadron Leader Grice, our tug pilot; arms and ammo and equipment checked once again. I remember vividly, drawing in chalk on the nose of Horsa HS 129 the insignia 'Wombat Mk1' and Vic writing his wife's name 'Sybil' on the other side. I remember one of the last things was to smear black, brown and green grease paint on our faces for camouflage. Then it seemed we were beside our glider and the ones who weren't going on this early lift were there saying cheerio and good luck. Good old Bill Fenge and of course, at the last minute, Lieutenant 'Tactical Tommy' Turner. A real character our Tommy—he hadn't been with the Squadron long, but had made quite an impression.

As a former instructor at the Southbourne Battle School, I was often employed on weapon training duties with the Squadron and when Lieutenant Tommy Turner arrived he sort of claimed me as his side-kick. He was an out and out fanatic on weapons and things that went bang! Young, about nineteen, and so fanatical that just prior to D-Day, he succeeded in blowing himself up with a hand grenade. When he knew that he'd blown his chances of the D-Day operation, he cried. Anyway, there he was swathed in bandages and splints saying goodbye and thrusting into my arms a huge wad of Noble's 808 plastic, a length of Cortex explosive and a bundle of detonators. 'Blow 'em sky high,' he called and then we were aboard and being tractored to our tug. Hooked up—a green, and at 23.20 or thereabouts we were off.

Sergeant Ron Bartley, also one of the 'A' Squadron pilots selected for the early lift, flew as second pilot to Staff Sergeant 'Jock' Bramah, and clearly remembers that last night at Harwell:

The fellows in the mess are knocking back the old wallop, but they are taking-off a day later than us. Young McManus (killed later at Arnhem) is kicking up a hell of a shindy because he has been left out of this operation. Absolutely sober myself and anyway, my stomach is just a frozen little knot which all the whisky in the world wouldn't penetrate. Time's getting on and we don the old battle outfit and go for final supper. This is an exclusive affair! Four crews, and what a smashing meal- bacon, eggs and the unusual constant attention of the cookhouse staff A few handshakes, but I never had much in common with these girls. Rather painful to have to walk right through the bar turning a deaf ear to the cries of 'Have a drink! '. The beer was always pretty bloody anyway, but we did have some good mess do's. Wrote a short letter home. It's difficult to say anything as we may be back in this country tomorrow. The truck arrives to take us around to the runway. We've always had to walk before! It's a lovely night and still light at 22.30. The gliders are marshalled on the east-west runway—big, black, ugly things. Why did I ever take up this game? Paint our faces black and say 'Hiya' to the two lads we are carrying along with the jeeps. Vic [Haines] says it will be a relief to get the thing over and join up at the ground rendezvous. Good bloke Vic—staunch, humorous—a very definite character. Griff [Major Billy Griffith] comes along and shakes hands with the usual good wishes.

As the four gliders and their Albemarle tugs, two from 570 Squadron and two from 295 Squadron RAF, took off and headed towards France, the thickening cloud and gathering darkness was a portent of the fate awaiting this group.

Chalk 67, flown by Staff Sergeant Billy Marfleet and Sergeant Vic Haines, had on board CQMS Albert Davies (9th Parachute Bn), Bombardier William Sidney (4th Airlanding Anti-Tank Bty RA) and Driver John Lunn (716 (Airborne) Lt Coy RASC) along with a jeep, trailer, four bikes, two bridging sections and several Bangalore Torpedoes. The equipment was vital to Colonel Terence Otway's plan to seize the Merville Battery. Flying Officer Christopher Lawson was the tug pilot:

> In approaching the French coast I flew into cloud at about 1500 ft. and immediately the glider started to dive and in so doing pulled up the nose of my aircraft. I asked the glider pilot if he could follow me satisfactorily and he replied "Yes", immediately afterwards, however, the glider dived again and the rope broke. It was estimated that at the time the combination was 2 miles off the coast. No explosion was seen on the water, so I assumed that the glider had reached the coast safely, or had made a good ditching just off shore.

Sadly, the glider had crashed into the water. All on board died as a result. The bodies of the passengers stayed together and they are buried in Ranville Cemetery. The bodies of Billy Marfleet and Vic Haines floated away from the wreckage. They were recovered from beaches a couple of days later. Billy Marfleet is buried in Bayeux and Vic Haines in Abbéville.

John Potts had been reassured by Lieutenant Irvine, the officer commanding the detachment of pathfinders from 22nd Independent Parachute Company, that his men would mark out the LZ:

> Lieutenant Irvine was an old Scottish international rugby player. He was a huge man and he had this habit of jabbing his short-stemmed pipe into his mouth and in a broad Scottish accent he said to myself and one or two others, 'Don't fear. Either the markers will be in place or I shall be dead.' It wasn't until 1985 that I learnt that he did die. He died on the drop.

At 0147 hours Bill Jones and John Potts took off from Brize Norton on a mission that was to turn out very differently from that envisaged by the planners of *Neptune*. All over southern England the skies reverberated to the sound of thousands of engines as the massed air fleet formed up ready for the crossing of the Channel.

Chapter Four

Shortly after midnight, the six *Coup de Main* gliders were approaching their release point. Their accurate arrival at the two tiny LZs would depend on precision stopwatch and compass flying with no second chance should an error be made. There was no moon that night, but the twin waters of the River Orne and the Caen Canal would be obvious from the air when the gliders got closer. However, in order not to alert the German garrisons at the bridges, the release point was further away than was normal on a glider operation. If the tugs released their charges at the wrong position then the glider pilots would not be able to find the LZs.

Major John Howard, the OC of the OBLI troops, had asked Staff Sergeant Jim Wallwork, the first pilot of Chalk 91, and his second pilot, Staff Sergeant John Ainsworth, to land the glider as close to the wire fence on the embankment by the bridge as they could manage. The Major was worried that any delay would lead to the Germans detonating demolition charges thought to be in place on the bridges. Wallwork and Ainsworth reassured Major Howard that they would do their best. The two pilots privately agreed that they would try to ram the nose of the glider through the fence. They were aware that at the very least this would mean broken legs for them both, the plywood and Perspex nose of the glider being unequal to the contest with the earth bank. Perhaps the two pilots considered this preferable to having the other two gliders ramming them from behind at high speed?

Private Denis Edwards, a passenger in Jim Wallwork's glider, takes up the story:

From a height of some six thousand feet we headed downwards at an ever increasing speed until we were within a thousand feet of the ground, then levelled out and glided more slowly downwards to make two sweeping right-hand turns before the final approach and run-in to the selected landing zone.

With our bodies taut, weapons gripped tightly, the senior pilot yelled 'Link arms' and we knew that at any moment we would touch down.

The time was now 0015 hours. We all held tight and braced ourselves for the landing. For about maybe forty or fifty yards we bumped forwards, bouncing in our wooden seats as the craft lost contact with the ground and came down again with another bump, a tug, a jerk and, for a few moments at least, it seemed as if we were in for a smooth landing.

As the thought flashed through my mind, the darkness suddenly filled with a stream of sparks as the underskids probably hit some stony ground. There was a sound like a giant sheet of cloth being ripped apart, then a God-almighty crash like a clap of thunder and my body seemed to be moving in different directions at the same time. The glider came to a juddering halt and I found myself at an uneven angle and peering into a blue-greyish haze. From somewhere outside tracer-like streams of multi-coloured light zoomed towards me.

The heavy landing had been partially a result of streaming the arrestor parachute. It had lifted the tail of the heavily over-loaded Horsa up and slammed the nose wheel into the ground, all three wheels being torn off by the contact with the earth. Denis Edwards and the other occupants of the glider were either dazed or knocked unconscious by the impact:

The noise ceased and was replaced with an ominous silence. Nothing and no-one moved. God help me we must be all dead, I thought. People began to stir in the glider's shattered interior. The door of the glider had been right beside my seat, but now all there was left was a mass of twisted wood and fabric and we had to smash our way out.

As I hit the ground I glanced quickly around from beneath the glider's tilted wing and immediately saw the canal swing bridge structure towering above me. The pilots had done a fantastic job, bringing the glider to a halt with its nose buried into a canal bank within about seventy-five yards of the bridge I glanced back at the glider and saw that the whole front had been smashed inwards, almost back to the wings, I had been sitting just below the forward edge of the wing. There had been some twenty feet of glider forward of my seat—now there was just a twisted mass of wreckage, I had been lucky but the two pilots and those in front of me must have been badly smashed up or killed. There was no time to stop and wonder. The job of my platoon was to fight our way across the bridge to the other side.

In fact both Wallwork and Ainsworth survived the landing. Wallwork had received a severe blow and cut to the head and was dazed but conscious, while Ainsworth had badly twisted his knee. Both men were still hospitalised on 20 June. In later years Jim Wallwork joked that he and

Ainsworth had been the first Allied soldiers to touch the soil of France. The crash had catapulted the two pilots, still strapped into their seats, through the Perspex cockpit canopy, head first into the embankment, trapping them under the wreckage of the front of the Horsa.

Staff Sergeant Oliver Boland and his second pilot, Staff Sergeant Bruce Hobbs, in Chalk 92 also landed correctly on LZ 'X', although they had only spotted the LZ from a height of two hundred feet, a superb feat of precision flying.

Boland mentioned in his official report that the glider was overloaded. This was a common problem with the Horsas that carried troops. The weight of the 'standard' infantryman was drastically underestimated. The number of men carried had been reduced before take-off when it was found that the engineers, who made up part of each platoon, carried even more kit than the infantry soldier. Each glider had reduced its complement of men by one. However, human nature had not been allowed for. All the troops were carrying extra ammunition and grenades—in one case a bucket full of Mills bombs! A bandolier of two hundred rounds of .303 ammunition weighed twelve pounds. Each glider carried twenty-eight troops, an extra weight penalty of many hundredweight.

The report on Operation *Tonga* (WO 171/1283 174049) completed by Major T. I. J. Toler, OC 'B' Squadron, states that 'Glider landed behind No. 91, but cockpit was also smashed on wire and Hobbs was cut about the legs, which he did not realise until two or three hours later when he was taken to the A.D.S. (Advanced Dressing Station).' Boland streamed the arrestor parachute on landing, but the glider was going too slowly for it to be effective.

Chalk 93 with Staff Sergeant Geoff Barkway and Sergeant Peter Boyle at the controls followed the other two gliders into the small LZ. Geoff Barkway, in an interview with Captain R. P. D. Folkes, Army Air Corps, described the run-in:

We settled down to fly the courses and looked for signs. I think we saw the wood, the Bois de Bavent. The water was where it should be—the river and the canal. That was on the right hand side and Peter had his lamp and he was giving me the courses and the times. Then I suppose it was as we turned into the last leg that almost simultaneously we both saw the bridge and the landing zone. We then set about getting it down. I don't remember seeing Oliver Boland, although he saw me.

We touched down and whether we hit right away .... I've a sort of idea that we didn't. We touched down and whipped along a bit, then this blooming thing -looked like a ditch or something—suddenly appeared and crash! That was it, out through the front! I remember laying there in the water thinking after two or three seconds, now come on this is not right! You've got to do something about this! So I sort of struggled up.

Fortunately the front had disintegrated so that the harness wasn't attached to anything, so there was no problem in getting free, but everything's a bit blurred after that, except that I have this thought that I got back into the glider for a stretcher. I don't know why I think that, but I do. Then at some time—this must have been all very quickly after we landed—a pain in the wrist. I remember seeing the poor fellow spread over the undercart, one of the chaps that was killed when we landed, his body straddled across the port undercarriage strut.

The 'poor fellow' on the undercarriage was Lance Corporal Fred Greenhalgh who had drowned in the pond. Lieutenant Smith, OC 14 Platoon, cut his head and the medical officer, Captain John Vaughan, RAMC, was badly concussed. Vaughan had been seated just behind the cockpit bulkhead and when the glider hit, he was catapulted through the bulkhead door, barely slowed by the Perspex windscreen, to land unconscious on the ground fifteen yards in front of the glider. Peter Boyle was trapped in the remains of the cockpit by his equipment. Geoff Barkway helped cut him free. The high speed of the glider's landing, about 90 to 100 mph, had contributed to the damage. Peter Boyle had been ferrying PIAT anti-tank launchers and grenades from the glider, which was now clearly illuminated by a German flare, up to the bridge, when he heard Geoff Barkway call out his name. Dashing back to the glider he found that his friend had been hit in the wrist with a bullet which had almost severed his arm. Barkway's next memory of that night was coming to in the aid post:

I was surrounded by everybody. I remember being very thirsty and being put on a stretcher across the bonnet of a jeep and being driven off somewhere. I can remember being on the beach. These were short little flashes and I must have been unconscious most of the time, because I think that the chaps on the beach had formed the opinion that that was the end of me when I went off to the aid post. They didn't give that much for my chances. On the beach we seemed to be under the frame of a lorry with a tarpaulin over it. Then I remember the tank landing ship, coming back in that and the incident of a petty officer getting a couple of sailors to lift me onto a bunk and tidying me up a bit. About the next thing I remember is the Sunday morning; being in Haslar Hospital. Well I didn't know till that Monday that I'd actually lost my arm because I had this feeling that I could move my fingers—a ghost limb. Patch it up, put it in a sling and suppose I'd be all right, only on the Monday morning when I suppose they came round to see how I was, I looked down and no arm! That caused quite a panic! I remember they doped me and knocked me out and on the Tuesday I had this haemorrhage and was whipped back down into the casualty ward. Being the only one in there I was surrounded by all these sick berth attendants and nursing sisters. There must have been about a dozen people and a rather luscious nurse was feeding me fish and chips and the left arm had the drip going into it when Eileen appeared.

The landing on LZ 'Y', the river bridge, did not go quite to plan. The first glider to land was Chalk 96, flown by Staff Sergeants Roy Howard and Fred Baacke. During the approach the pilots found that they could not get the speed of the Horsa below 90 mph. Roy Howard sent two of the soldiers to the rear of the glider and found that this reduced the speed to 80 mph. It landed with only the nose wheel broken, close to the bridge, in the LZ. Roy Howard commented on the landing:

> I first saw the bridge at 800 feet and was able to land in the correct place without damaging the glider, or the troops inside it. We had been fitted with an emergency parachute brake, but I had no need to use this I was surprised, just before touch-down, to see a herd of cows in the field. I think the cows were more surprised than I was and they quickly ran away. I shouted back into the glider, 'You're in the right place,' and Mr Fox quickly led his men out.

Lieutenant Fox and 17 Platoon attacked and took the bridge with little opposition, the pilots helping casualties to the R.A.P.

Staff Sergeants Stan Pearson and Len Guthrie in Chalk 95 had insufficient height to reach the LZ and landed in a field five hundred yards north of the bridge. By the time that Lieutenant Sweeney and 23 Platoon reached it, 17 Platoon were triumphant. The third glider for LZ 'Y', Chalk 94, flown by Staff Sergeants Lawrence and Shorter suffered a greater woe. The tug mistook the estuary of the Dives for the Orne and released them in the 'wrong place. They landed near a bridge over the Dives a mile to the east of Harcouel and captured that one. This glider carried 22 Platoon, under Lieutenant Hooper and the 2IC, Captain Priday.

Hooper and Shorter were sent to a farmhouse to recce. Finding the coast clear, Hooper sent Shorter back for the platoon. Meanwhile the Germans arrived and captured Hooper, who was sent back up the road with two escorts. The two glider pilots and Captain Priday ambushed the Germans, who were quickly shot, and released the platoon commander. The party made their way back towards the Ranville area, gathering assorted lost souls from the various parachute drops *en route*. Although not everything had gone according to plan, the operation was a great success. Both objectives were taken intact and the gliders had proved their effectiveness against a pinpoint target. The conduct of the pilots was exemplary and Hobbs, Howard, Pearson and Wallwork were awarded DFMs for their part in the operation.

Around 2300 hours on D-Day the unwounded pilots were dispatched towards the beaches, the bridges now reinforced by elements of the 1st Special Service Brigade. Major Howard had been ordered by Brigadier Nigel Poett not to risk the lives of the pilots in combat against ground forces, as it had been planned to use them in another massed landing behind German lines should the Invasion become bogged down at the beach-head. In recognition of the task accomplished by the troops and the glider pilots the canal bridge was, and still is, named 'Pegasus Bridge' and the river bridge, 'Horsa Bridge'.

The other early landings of *Tonga* were not to go so smoothly. Six gliders from 'F' Squadron were to land on LZ 'K' with jeeps and explosives for 8th Parachute Battalion's Engineers, which would be used to destroy the bridges over the Dives and La Divette. Seven gliders from 'E' Squadron were to land on LZ 'V' with the Headquarters of 3rd Parachute Brigade, personnel from 1st (Canadian) Parachute Battalion and a couple of six-pounder anti-tank guns On the same LZ four 'A' Squadron Horsas would bring in the heavy equipment that Terence Otway needed to seize Merville. As the attack was underway it was planned that three gliders carrying soldiers from 'A' Company, 9th Parachute Battalion would land inside the perimeter of the Battery itself. To guide the parachutists and gliders onto the correct DZs and LZs pathfinders would set up Eureka beacons and Holophane lights. The timing of the sticks from 22 Independent Company was extremely tight. Private Frank Ockenden:

We were trained in the use of Eureka-Rebecca and Glim Light. The Eureka was radar equipment that sent out a signal so that the pilots of the tug aircraft, which was fitted with Rebecca, homed-in on it to release the gliders or drop parachutists on the LZ or DZ. Like everything else it was very fragile and very easily damaged when dropped and should have been treated with more care. A lot of the trouble that arose on the LZ and DZ was the fault of the ground staff back in England through lack of maintenance. A lot of the batteries were no good and we were not to know until the last minute, which in a lot of cases was too late.

A lot of blame has been put on the Pathfinders but under the circumstances I know they did a first-class job. Nothing was said to us at briefing about the flooding in the area of the River Dives. The reconnaissance flights must have picked it up! I was in one of two sticks that were to be dropped to mark out DZ 'K', under the command of Major Payne. The Albemarle we flew in was a bloody awful aircraft. It carried twelve men and you had to squeeze tight up to the top gunner, not like the Dakota that carried more men much more comfortably! As we flew over the Channel the sky seemed to become lighter and the waves were breaking over the shore as we passed over the coast. Gunfire was making little red blobs in front of us but we could not hear a thing because of the engines. When the red light came on we were already hooked up in case of a hit by flak, but so far it was no worse than flying in a thunder storm. Someone said five minutes to DZ. We all stood up and took up positions ready to jump. This was it! No turning back and no calling it off this time. Someone shouted 'Green light on! Good luck boys.' I thought we would need it. Out of the plane we went. Done it lots of times—just like dropping on' Salisbury Plain.

Hit the ground with a bump. I never saw it as we came in lower and lower, the ground got darker. No damage done so I got out of my chute and looked around. It didn't look like any of the models or maps we had studied for hours. Found Tommy Green, but nothing of Taffy Burt. Heard heavy gunfire to my right and guessed it came from Caen. Tommy was doing a recce and when he came back I told him that I thought we were in the wrong place. We then heard planes and down floated some Paras. A sergeant came running over. 7th Battalion, mate?' he said. 'No. 8th,' I replied. 'Bloody Hell, they've dropped us in the wrong place,' he said. He was okay, it was us in the wrong place. We worked our way over in the direction of Troarn towards the LZ. When we got there it was pandemonium. There were aircraft going in all directions over the DZ. What a balls-up! When I got there I bent over the Eureka to activate it when something hit me on the back of the head. Tommy told me later that a lad from the 13th Battalion had knocked me out with his boots as he was coming in to land by parachute. We saw one glider land and REs running all over the place with a Polish trolley. Guess it must have been Major Roseveare's men who were to blow the bridge at Troarn. Just as we made our way to the woods we saw a glider come straight down nose first and hit the ground about 80mph. It just scattered all over the place—never saw anyone left alive.

The Pathfinders had been scattered all over the area. In the thirty minutes available before the main drops were due to land, small groups desperately tried to identify their whereabouts and reach their allocated positions. Not many made it to the right place at the right time. Private Arthur Platt, a Pathfinder attached to the recce party of 8th Battalion was caught by the Germans as he was laying flares for one of the Horsas due to land at LZ

'K'. He was executed on the spot with a bullet through the back of the neck. One Pathfinder had his Eureka beacon strapped to the outside of his leg, as he boarded the aircraft, with the detonator handle in the 'primed' position. Once extended this could not be retracted without the internal demolition charge exploding. Needless to say the subsequent parachute landing worked to the detriment of both beacon and leg! Over half the Pathfinders were dropped in the wrong place, one team only sixteen minutes before the main drop. Almost all the beacons and Holophane lights for 'V' were damaged or missing. One team for LZ 'K' were dropped on 'N' and not realising their error, they set up their beacons. To compound these problems, the only two working lights for LZ 'V' were set up in standing crops and therefore not visible to the pilots in the dropping aircraft.

Decades later, accusation and counter-accusation still raged over who should take the blame for the poor marking of the DZs and LZs on these initial phases of *Tonga*. On the face of it though, it does seem strange that the RAF should accuse the Pathfinders of poor navigation skills when they were dropped in the wrong place to begin with. A case of 'the chicken and the egg'! It is easy, with hindsight, to criticise. In practice, a night operation of this scale and complexity is notoriously difficult to get right, especially with the technology of 1944.

While the Pathfinder teams struggled to do their job, the gliders of Wave Two were nearing the French coast.

Chapter Five

The seven gliders from 'E' Squadron tasked for LZ 'V' had taken off from Down Ampney at about 2240 hours. The Horsa of Lieutenant Chris Dodwell, commanding the detachment, and Sergeant B. Osborne, were towed by Wing Commander Maurice Booth of 271 Squadron. As they formed up over England, Dodwell could see the Thames glinting faintly below them in the last of the light:

> We then flew a south-easterly course towards Worthing, where we would cross the English coast. The tug aircraft was equipped with the 'Gee' type of navigation equipment, which was capable of plotting its position with considerable accuracy. However, even before we crossed the coast, I heard over the telephone line, which ran inside the tow-rope, that the Gee set had broken down.
>
> In this situation Maurice Booth decided to aim for Le Havre and the Seine estuary, which would provide a landmark and then fly westwards along the French coast and hope to identify the point along which we were due to cross it and then turn in. Flying along the coast might expose us to anti-aircraft fire, but we would have to hope for the best. Our altitude would be 2500 feet, at which height, the light anti-aircraft guns of the Germans would be firing at their extreme range, while we would be too low for the heavy guns to be accurate.
>
> As we crossed the English coast the weather conditions began to deteriorate. Low clouds obscured the moon, which was only about half-full anyway, and the wind increased. Below, we could see dimly, a grey and not very pleasant-looking sea. Fortunately, as a result of problems during some of our night training exercises, I had persuaded Maurice Booth to have his system of lights on the tug wingtips and tail modified, so that he could turn them up from their normal dim setting to a greater brightness for bad conditions. If the glider got too far out of position behind the tug the tow-rope would break and this indeed happened to a number of gliders over the Channel that night. However, in our case

being able to call Maurice up for more light when necessary, enabled us to keep reasonable station, though sometimes it was hard work.

At last we sighted the Seine estuary and turned westward. The coastal towns were, of course, all blacked out and the only lights we could see were the little pinpoints of fire from anti-aircraft guns. Fortunately, they were having difficulty in getting our range, or their predictors couldn't cope with our low speed. The first landmark visible was the River Touques which runs into the Channel at Deauville. The next was the River Dives at Houlgate/Cabourg. Then very quickly we reached the point at which we had to turn inland towards our designated landing zone. We were reasonably sure that we had the right point, or very close to it, but as soon as we crossed the coast we found that we had to contend with thick clouds of smoke and dust. This was the result of the heavy bombing of the German coastal battery at Merville, which had just taken place.

Nothing could be distinguished clearly on the ground. The only thing that Maurice could do was to fly on the correct bearing for so many minutes as he calculated would bring us to the right spot. When he said over the telephone line, 'This is it' we had to make a very rapid decision. The ground was barely visible and certainly no landing lights put out by the advance party of parachutists were visible. Given the atrocious conditions in the area there seemed to be little point in asking the tug to make a circuit, and indeed that would make our position more uncertain still. Hoping for the best I reached forward and pulled the lever which released the tow-rope and left us in free flight. We lost height steadily.

My second pilot was calling out the height every hundred feet as we came down. At 500 feet we began to distinguish some of the features on the ground, but none of the landmarks we had memorised showed up and there were none of the guiding lights on which we had so much to depend. Somewhere below us a German gun was firing tracer. At 300 feet I could see a small open space among the surrounding trees and orchards. We headed towards this. As we came closer I could see that there was a row of tall trees along its edge. Since the field was a small on we would have to go through the tops of the trees to get in.

Everyone braced themselves for the landing. As the ground rushed up we suddenly saw in front of us, obstruction poles placed there by the Germans to deter glider landings. The first few we managed to steer between, at the cost of some damage to our wings. Then, just as we were coming to a halt, the last pole came through the front of the cockpit.

It was fortunate that by this time our speed was so low, or things would have been much worse. Even so, my second pilot, Osborne, gave a cry of pain and the cockpit was filled with the hissing of compressed air escaping from the ruptured air bottles, which provided the power to work the flaps.

Osborne's left ankle was badly damaged, but we got him out and made him as comfortable as we could. Leaving him as our lookout, we took stock of the Horsa. It was lying half on its side and down by the nose. Our flight had lasted some two hours and five minutes. The time was now about one a.m.'

They were down two miles short of the LZ.

The second 271 Dakota to take-off was skippered by Major Joubert. He was towing Chalk 262, flown by Staff Sergeant A. N. 'Andy' Andrews, DFM, and Sergeant Paddy Senier. Inside Andrew's glider were two wireless-equipped ambulance jeeps and their drivers from HQ 3rd Parachute Brigade. He had also been entrusted to carry Brigadier Hill's personal kit, a responsible task indeed! Unlike the Dakota of Maurice Booth, they were not dogged by equipment failure. Flight Lieutenant Ralph Fellows, the map reader in the tug noted:

We flew at about 1200 feet and the trip to the English coast was uneventful. The 'Gee' Chain worked beautifully and we maintained our track perfectly. Crossing the English Channel we relied on Gee, of course, but we had no doubts and this was confirmed when we saw the coast of France ahead of us. While still a few miles off shore we could see a number of familiar landfalls and all was well.

It was at this juncture that Bomber Command entered the picture. Quite suddenly the coast ahead erupted in the bursting of bombs and the flashes from A.A. batteries. Just as suddenly, it seemed, the coastline disappeared as we flew into a cloud of smoke and debris.

The smoke from the bombing raid had been quite worrying for Andy Andrews in the glider:

The smoke got thicker and demanded extreme concentration on the part of the tug pilot, Paddy, and myself. We didn't fancy landing in the Channel at any time, especially this night. Paddy was talking over the intercom and I tried to observe the lights on the wings of the tug, Just when everything was disappearing and I was preparing to go into the low-tow position, the smoke gradually began to clear until, quite suddenly, we were in comparatively good night visibility. Almost at once the Observer, speaking as calmly as if he was ordering another beer, said 'Oh there are the two houses—bang on time too.' This was very comforting and a great relief. The flak was coming up lazily but didn't seem interested in us until just before the tracer burnt out. Almost unconsciously Paddy, who was flying now, skidded away slightly out of position, but he soon corrected and I concentrated on finding those lights.

Our normal practice was to let Paddy fly the glider until I was quite certain of my landmarks, then I would say goodbye to the tug and take over for the landing. Between us we had calculated that at the operational height and the time of crossing the coast, between the two houses we should fly at approximately ninety seconds before pulling off, and then whether the lights were visible or not we could fly straight ahead and land within reach of our rendezvous. Well the best made plans do seem to go astray.

There were no lights! In a voice which sounded rather unreal I could hear myself asking Major Joubert about it and he, in a very cheery manner, replying, 'Don't worry, hang on, we have bags of time, I'll go round again in a second or two'.

Ralph Fellows and the tug pilot had made contingency plans should all not go as expected:

Major Joubert and I had agreed that in case the 'T' lights were not there, or not visible to us, we should have an alternative pin-point. This was to be a wood, roughly square in shape but hollow in the middle. We figured if all else failed that this should be our point of release. At the time when we in the tug could see the wood ahead, we still had not seen the 'T'. Almost at our wood Major Joubert saw some lights to our right and passed this information to Andy.

Andy Andrews was aware that this LZ was not 'V', but was about the same distance from the coast. He asked the Major to fly a little to the right and made a quick decision:

Within five seconds it was just the right spot, I said goodbye, and someone wished us luck, and then there was the familiar jerk with the noise of the wind gradually receding to the background, the speed dropping off to a more modest 80mph. Paddy had handed over the controls and was intently watching an ack-ack battery on our right, whose tracer seemed a bit too near. He drew my attention to it and almost at once, as I put on half flap, the flak turned and seemed to have found another target. Then we saw the target, another Horsa, well below us, flying towards the flak. Just a second afterwards it switched its emergency lights on and illuminated a small row of trees between ourselves and the 'T' along which it was flying. I had to forget it then, but Paddy said later it seemed to crash into some trees to the right of the 'T' along which it was flying. Then we were coming in just right. A little bump, and then another, something like a ditch I thought. Then a wheel seemed to stick and start to swing the glider round. I applied full opposite rudder and my brake quickly, and no sooner had we straightened up than we stopped. I heaved a sigh and then immediately shot out of my seat; we were on the first light and not in our correct position on the extreme left of the 'T'. Having been forewarned by a training mishap that this might happen; we had arranged that Paddy would jump out and wave his torch to show the rear of the glider. This he did with feverish haste. I collected our personal kit and rifles and jumped out. The two 'bods', whom I had completely forgotten about, were on the ground before me. They took up positions on either side of the glider while I went round to Paddy.

We got ready to beat a hasty retreat if another glider was coming in on top of us, but there was not a sign of anything in the sky. You have no doubt been at an appointed place at the right time, waited for someone to arrive, and had to go away in disgust.

We felt like that at first. Then a feeling of loneliness crept over us; even the Germans didn't greet us! Where were the Independent Parachutists who had put the 'T' out? Not a soul, not a noise, nothing.

Warrant Officer Don Wood flew the last of the glider-towing Dakotas to take off from Down Ampney that night. He towed Chalk 267, piloted by Staff Sergeant Vic Saunders and Sergeant John Fuell. Don Wood's Dakota was not fitted with 'Gee' and the poor visibility and strong crosswind made navigation demanding:

> The weather was very bad and so we flew at 600 to 700 feet for the most part, occasionally coming down to 500 feet as we were in and out of the cloud bottoms. With the thick cloud above there was neither starlight nor moonlight to assist and it was pitch black. We had been briefed to look for a Holophane light, which should have been placed at the coast crossing point and this would have assisted us greatly. Whether such a light had been placed we never did find out, but not one of the crews saw it and so we relied almost entirely on time to tell us when to release. We had also hoped to be able to see some sort of a line of surf on the coast but this was never seen as the light was so poor. Just as time was up I got the impression of a vague change in darkness underneath and thought that this was land. I called for the glider to release, which was done immediately. At the same time my co-pilot Sergeant Tyler, pointed out to starboard and we saw another glider very close to us, also free on its way down.

This glider could have been Chalk 266, flown by Staff Sergeant Bill Herbert and Sergeant Gerry Moorcraft. Towed by Pilot Officer Don Williams it landed straddling a country lane near Varaville, close to, but not on, the LZ. Alternatively, it may have been Chalk 264 of Staff Sergeant Gardner and Sergeant Oliver which landed in three feet of water near Briqueville in the flooded Dives valley, only one and a half miles south of the LZ. Unfortunately both pilots from this glider were captured. Whichever one of the gliders it was, it didn't affect the fate of Saunders and Fuell, whose Horsa, heavily laden with jeep, six-pounder anti-tank gun and ammunition, crashed on landing, seven miles to the south-east of the LZ. The two pilots and the gun commander, Lance Sergeant Woodcock, were killed instantly, all three later laid to rest in the war cemetery at Lisieux. With the visibility being what it was, and given the manoeuvring ability of a laden Horsa, by the time the crew saw what was ahead of them, it would have been next to impossible to avoid it.

Gunner W. Jones was one of the two survivors from the crash:

> I do not know what happened while we were in the air, I know that we were loose from the plane was gliding down when we went into a dive, which we never came out of. When I recovered I made my way around the Glider, the first man I found was my own Sgt Woodcock he was quite dead. Then one of the pilots which one I could not say as they had blacked there [sic] faces and I had not met them before we took to loading the Glider. He also was dead. I looked for the other pilot, but of him I could find no trace, and I thought he must have been thrown into a wood at the side of were [sic] we crashed. ..I had to leave then, I had one mate with me a Gnr Paget, I told him that 2 were dead and I could not find the other.

It is more than likely that Jones and Paget survived because they were in the tail of the glider, behind the six pounder gun and its jeep. They did not remain at large for long, and spent the rest of the War in *Stalag* IV-B.

The glider of Staff Sergeant H. 'Lofty' Rancom and Sergeant Collard, number 265, was towed by Flight Lieutenant Jimmy Edwards, the comedian. He had flown up and down the coast from Ouistreham to Le Havre in an attempt to find the LZ. Eventually, due to lack of fuel, he had to cast off the glider, which landed in a minefield, within a 'defended' area. Rancom, whose arm was badly injured, and Collard hid up for a few days before deciding to make their, way to Paris. It was on this journey that an SS unit captured them. Both men survived the war but Lofty Rancom lost his arm.

Of the seven 'E' Squadron gliders only one, that of Staff Sergeant J. 'Taffy' Lovett and Sergeant J. 'Tug' Wilson landed on LZ 'V'. The four Harwell gliders fared even worse. Staff Sergeant Marfleet's glider was already down in the Channel, with no survivors.

Sergeant Ron Bartley was second pilot to Staff Sergeant Maurice 'Jock' Bramah in Chalk 69, which was carrying two jeeps and two men of No. 3 Section, 224 Parachute Field Ambulance:

We were on the track that led to the landing zone, but when we were some miles off the Normandy coast we ran into flak and a patch of dense cloud, or smoke. Everything went haywire and I felt a twang as the tow-rope broke. This was bad! A second later we came out of the cloud but could see no sign of the land at all.

Gave the order to prepare for ditching and JB was at the controls in a jiffy. I was out of my seat and started to hack an escape hole through the roof of the fuselage. I shouted to the two passengers to do the same and hardly had the words left my mouth when the noise of their hacking came to my ears. Fear lent speed to our actions and the cutting was well under way when JB shouted that he could see the coastline and also thought that we could make it. I returned to the cockpit just in time to see the coastline disappearing underneath us I could distinguish the houses on the seafront and one or two bursts of tracer greeted us, passing through the starboard wing. I could now see nothing but woods underneath and it looked as if a crash landing was inevitable. It was straight into an orchard with an airspeed of around 100 mph.

I can't recollect the actual landing, though I'm sure I didn't lose consciousness, for when I began to take note, I was on the ground with the cockpit crushed into matchwood above me, still creaking as it settled.

Their glider had landed in woods above Villers-sur-Mer, well away from the LZ.

The closest glider to the LZ was that of Staff Sergeant Ernie Thorpe and Sergeant Bob Hardie. This landed heavily three-quarters-of-a mile to the south-west of LZ 'V', badly injuring Hardie in the crash, as he describes:

We pulled off and undershot, landing in the field before the LZ and hitting the trees which divided the two fields. l was in the co-pilot's seat which made contact with a tree trunk, taking me through the bulkhead and finishing up with control wires wrapped round my legs and arms. This resulted in me having three fractures in my right leg and a fractured right arm. They strapped me to a branch and put me in a ditch. Ernie later returned with a stretcher party and I was taken to a field hospital. It was a year before I returned to duty with the Regiment.

Chalk 66, piloted by Staff Sergeants Vic Ockwell and Ron Hellyer, had on board Lieutenant J. S. Robinson, Driver G. H. Fuller, Mr Fyffe a War

Correspondent with the *Daily Mirror*, a Jeep, trailer, four bicycles, twenty Bangalore Torpedoes and two foot bridges. These latter were being counted on by Colonel Otway to cross over the anti-tank ditch of the Merville Battery. The tug pilot, Squadron Leader Grice, recalled the crossing:

> The weather was fine and the visibility good all the way across the English Channel. Within about three miles of the French coast a belt of low cloud was encountered. Bumpiness in the cloud was very violent and almost immediately the rope broke and the glider disappeared from sight. Until then communication between tug and glider had been maintained and all was going very well. Owing to the low cloud and the nearness of the French coast it was impossible to make any attempt to search for the glider.

Ron Hellyer also remembers the problems caused by the bombing raid on the battery by the Lancasters:

> We were completely engulfed in thick black smoke and were being battered by gale force winds. Our tug had vanished from view and I know that our pitching and rolling and yawing must have made his Albemarle's flying attitude impossible. Whether Gricey released us or our tow-rope broke, I'll never know, but suddenly we were in free flight. Vic grabbed the controls and released our tow-rope. There was no panic—we were too well trained for that. As we were still over the sea, I left my seat and told our troops to stand by for ditching. l picked up our fire axe and as Vic nodded in agreement, I hacked away at the cockpit screen in front of me. This action, l believe implicitly, was what saved my life. All this took less time than it's taken to write about. Regaining my seat and strapping myself in, l noticed that we were just crossing from sea to land at about 900 feet and ASI of 80–85 mph.
>
> To port and above us was an Albemarle climbing steeply and banking to port with a line of tracer shells chasing it. No doubt it was Squadron Leader Grice.
>
> Beneath us were concrete fortifications, fields and hedges and thin lines of green and red tracer glancing up at us. Vic was as calm as usual and flying straight and level whilst we were both searching for recognisable objects or even a lighted LZ. We could not be far from our LZ providing we hadn't lost our course after our tow parted.
>
> Being over land I shouted back to the troops to cancel ditching and prepare for a crash landing. Someone was standing in the doorway and I told him to get the hell back in no uncertain terms. We were now at about 400 feet and Vic suddenly applied flap and I saw we were headed

for what looked like a ploughed field. Now if Lady Luck hadn't deserted us we would have made a decent, if somewhat bumpy, landing. Vic, superb, unflappable Vic, was in complete control. I don't think either of us was frightened at all tense and excited perhaps, but it was just like lots of other approaches we had made in England. Knowing it could be a bit rough, l folded my arms in front of my face. Nothing was said—we had a gale blowing in through the shattered Perspex which deafened us. Then it seemed as if hell had broken loose. Our port wing must have fouled an anti-landing post, or some other immovable object. The aircraft slewed violently to port and bashed its nose into the ground. The noise of splintering and crashing was horrendous and then I knew nothing more. I could only have been unconscious a short time because—and honestly, I don't know whether this is fact of fantasy—I opened my eyes and there were two glider pilots standing looking down at me. They were both wearing those hideous skull crash helmets we had and both were wearing Denison smocks. They started to move away and I called out 'Vic, help me Vic'. Or did I? Or was it fantasy? I'll never know because I never saw him again. I tried to get up but I couldn't move and I thought 'God, my spine's broken'. Then I must have passed out again for a few moments.

The non-arrival of these gliders for LZ 'V' was to test both Colonel Otway's and 3 Parachute Battalion's resources severely.

The six gliders of 14 Flight, 'F' Squadron, who were to land on LZ 'K', had a mixed result. Five carried explosives for Major Tim Roseveare's engineers to blow up bridges over the River Dives. The sixth carried a medical jeep, trailer and medics of 224 Parachute Field Ambulance.

Lieutenant Aubrey Pickwoad, OC 14 Flight, and Sergeant Michael Watts were in the lead glider. Aubrey Pickwoad recalled:

Somehow we had got off course a bit to port and could just make out the French coast when rather heavy anti-aircraft fire opened up on us, apparently from Le Havre. Anyway, they were a bit off target, so we altered course to starboard, heading for Ouistreham and as we crossed the coast, we could see a great cloud of smoke caused by the RAF bombing the coastal guns. We were now at 1500 feet so, with the moonlight, one could see the ground quite clearly. We had worked out the time of flight from the coast to LZ 'K' before take-off, so stopwatch was set on crossing the coast. After a few minutes a beacon could be seen flashing to port. It was rather difficult to make out if it was 'N' (dash-dot) or 'K' (dash-dot-dash), the dashes and dots were too close together.

The two LZs ('K' and 'N') were only about three miles apart and a similar distance in from the coast. Aubrey Pickwoad believes that this might have been the cause of three of his six gliders landing on LZ 'N' by mistake, although he thinks that they should have realised that the timing was wrong, and searched for the correct LZ. However, if the gliders crossed the coast at the incorrect point then the timings would be out anyway. It is also possible that these crews were homing into the 'K' beacon mistakenly set up on LZ 'N' by the pathfinders.

Pickwoad realised that the first LZ he saw was not 'K':

A few seconds later the real 'K' could be seen on the port side. I could also make out the crossroad in the middle of the common. I called to the tug pilot, thanked him for a good flight, bade him farewell and released. I flew over the beacon and side-slipped to port to lose height. In doing so I saw another glider, which turned out to be that flown by Staff Sergeant R. Banks and Sergeant B. Hebblethwaite. The last photos we had showed the Jerries had been planting poles in the possible LZs, so I went down to about 100 feet and approached the beacon to my right as I was not sure of how far the poles were planted. I flicked on my landing light and landed safely in one piece, Staff Sergeant Banks coming after me and landing about a hundred yards behind.

Staff Sergeant Bill Ridgeway and Sergeant Peter Foster were piloting Chalk 220. A Missing Personnel report on Foster recorded:

Released from Tug 1500' height just South landing area TOUFFREVILLE (nr TROARN), turned in right direction to land on landing area, but no more seen. No crash reported and no wreckage found. Situation did not permit search. Time 0045 hrs.

The glider in fact landed five miles south-east of LZ 'K' in the flooded marshes (Le Marais de Vimont) close to the village of Vimont, which also happened to be the HQ of 21st Panzer Divsion Commander Hans von Luck. On board were passengers Driver Douglas Knappett RASC, Sergeant D. Jeffreys and Privates W. Osbourne and W. G. Southerton, all of 8th Parachute Battalion. In addition to the explosives, the glider also carried Vickers machine guns, 3-inch mortars and ammunition.

The occupants were looked after by locals. During an attempt to get to Allied lines Foster was shot and killed. The passengers escaped and Ridgway made it back to safety. He was captured during another attempt.

The remaining three gliders all landed on LZ 'N'.

Staff Sergeant Laurie Weeden, in Chalk 223 with Sergeant S. Griffiths:

I think, with the benefit of hindsight, that we must have crossed the coast about two miles west of the correct course, and though we landed successfully at grid 126737 on LZ 'N', we were about two and a half miles from LZ 'K', close to the village of Ranville.

He also believes that another possibility was that the tug pilots may have been looking at 'K' while the glider crews may have been seeing 'N'. When Weeden heard, over the intercom, Warrant Officer' Zombie' McRae's sighting of a flare path over to port, he released the tow-rope:

I turned on to a south-easterly course and, with height to lose, applied full flap and headed for a landing to the starboard side of the beacon, fortuitously coming to a halt close to a line of trees which effectively would have barred any further progress. In the landing the nosewheel assembly in the cockpit had been damaged, but fortunately the glider was straight and level for unloading purposes.

It was later confirmed that, due to the misleading landing aid, Laurie Weeden had been landing downwind with a 27 knot wind on his tail.

The suitability of LZs 'K' and 'V' has been the subject of controversy for many years among the pilots. The site of LZ 'V' had been changed at the last minute and then changed back again. Colonel G. J. S. Chatterton, DSO, in *Commander Glider Pilots Appreciation of the Situation—Operations Tonga and Mallard* had this to say about LZ 'V':

The area is almost totally prepared for obstruction .... only one suitable area, which is 1000 yards from DZ. This area is .... roughly circular with a thick rectangular wood to the north. The total length is nearly 1000 yards and its width 500 yards. For the eleven gliders in LZ 'V' a large unobstructed field was chosen after work of obstruction of the previously selected LZ had commenced. The field was not acceptable to the GOC 6 Airborne Div owing to the distance, some thousand yards from the parachute DZ. A similar difficulty arose in the case of 'K' where no suitable area free from the preparation of obstruction could be found north of a line already enumerated in my letter dated24th May 1944. After study of the latest air cover, from which it would appear that the poles were not at that time—28th May 1944—actually expected, and a conference with the GOC 6 Airborne Div in which the necessity for support by the glider loads of 6 Pdr guns was stressed, I have agreed that the landings shall remain as originally planned. I have made 6 Airborne Div aware however that I consider these phases of the Operation have only a limited chance of success, dependent almost entirely on the existing state of the obstruction.

Report on Operations and Photographic Results. VIII, App. 2 (WO 171/1230) has this conclusion about LZ 'V':

> This operation was always considered extremely difficult. A landing zone had to be found without markers in difficult country. It is considered that the original field chosen would have been easier as it was dark and distinctive.

Colonel Chatterton's doubts about the successful outcome of this phase of the operation seem to have been swept under the table by Gale. The main reasons for the number of gliders which missed the LZs seem to be a combination of poor visibility, as a direct result of the Lancaster raid on the Merville Battery, a lack of clear marking with 'Eureka' and Holophane lights on both LZs and navigation problems experienced by the tugs. Those equipped with serviceable 'Gee' seemed to have few problems keeping to the correct track. For those not so fortunate, there was a long flight across the sea, which did not allow much chance to observe drift caused by side winds, followed by the need to find and cross the coast at a precise spot in poor visibility. It should be noted that the wind direction given at briefing was approximately 180 degrees. In their Glider Raid Reports, Warrant Officer Berry and Warrant Officer Bain, both of 298 Squadron RAF, gave the wind direction, and speed at approximately 0020 hours, as 309 degrees/28 knots and 312 degrees/18 knots. This evidence is supported by another thirty-two reports from tug pilots from later waves, the wind gusting up to 35 knots and veering to 320 degrees. Together, these factors caused a wide dispersal of the glider landings. It was now up to the men on the ground to make the most of their situation and get the job done.

There has been much debate, some of which has been quite acrimonious, about the identity, even the existence of, the so-called 'Mystery Glider' of Merville. Alan R. Jefferson's book, *Assault on the Guns of Merville*, mentions the crash landing of a glider near Number 4 Casement at 0145 hours British time. A senior German NCO, Sergeant-Major Buskotte, described the vicious fight which ensued between the Battery garrison and the occupants of the glider, who were not inclined to surrender. Eventually all the occupants of the glider were killed in the hand-to-hand fighting. It is this supposition that all occupants were killed that has caused the credibility problem, as it is known that there were survivors in all the craft which could have been candidates for 'mystery glider'. However, if some of the glider crew survived and evaded capture, then Buskotte would not have been aware of their existence. In his eyes, there would indeed have been no survivors.

There is only one glider, out of the seventeen which were landing around that time, which cannot be discounted—that of Staff Sergeant Rancom and Sergeant Collard. The landing sites of all the other gliders can be accounted for. Many of the circumstances described by Rancom fit in with recent evidence supplied by Buskotte, who cannot have had access to Rancom's story, which has never been published. This was told to Andy Andrews some years after the War by Lofty Rancom himself.

Major Mike Strong, the curator of the Merville Battery Museum, interviewed the German, and he is convinced that the former Sergeant-Major is a reliable witness and is telling the truth. The two men walked the ground of the Battery, Buskotte pointing out the exact position that the glider landed. This spot agrees with Rancom's description of his landing area—mined and within a defended area. It is very probable that the 'Mystery Glider' was Chalk 265.

Chapter Six

No sooner had the gliders come to a halt on the ground, than the pilots changed roles. Each crew had been briefed in detail as to its job on the ground. Once the contents of the gliders had been off-loaded the crews then became fighting soldiers.

However, for many crews, the first problem was how to get the load out of the glider. Chris Dodwell, Chalk 261:

The method of unloading the jeep and trailer we were carrying was to undo a series of bolts which held on the whole tail section of the glider. This tail section would then fall off, enabling the crew to fix in place two lengths of steel channelling, down which the jeep could then be driven to the ground. We set to the business of undoing the bolts but found them immovable. We kept on with our efforts for a considerable time, but to no avail. It seemed that the damage done by the obstruction poles during our landing had jammed things.

We then decided to try to unload via the side ramp. This was a hinged section of fuselage which could be lowered. It meant we had to get the trailer out first and then the jeep. We got the heavily loaded trailer onto the side ramp but, because of the angle at which the glider was lying, we could not prevent it breaking away and overturning at the foot of the ramp.

There were only four of us—myself and the three signallers. Osborne, with his injured ankle, was quite unable to help. It seemed that we would need more help to get the jeep unloaded and the trailer righted. Just at this moment, there appeared overhead a line of Dakotas flying low. The visibility had improved by now and I was able to see that they were not towing gliders, so they must be on a parachute drop. All the Dakotas carrying parachutists had their side doors removed and I could also see that there were no static lines trailing from the doorways. This meant that they had not yet dropped their parachutists. With my compass I took the bearing of their direction.

We had no accurate idea of where we were. Only one thing was certain—
we were not in the precise spot where we had intended to be. We were
going to need assistance to get the glider unloaded. The best bet would be
to meet up with the parachute forces which had just passed overhead. In
training we had practised night marches by compass. We started out on the
bearing I had taken, keeping as far as possible, to the cover of hedgerows
and ditches. I detailed one of the signallers to help the injured Osborne
at the rear. We made frequent stops to check our bearings and to ensure
that we were all there. After some time we came out on to a minor road,
which led us towards a village. Rather than go through the middle, we
made a circuit around it through gardens and orchards. This was just as
well, as I discovered later on, that the village was Breville, which was full
of German troops. Sometime after passing Breville we found that, in the
darkness, we had lost touch with Osborne. We cast back along our track
but could not find him and reluctantly, we had to resume our march. We
continued along a road which ran in approximately the right direction and
by now there were the first glimmerings of light. As we came to a small set
of crossroads, which I discovered later on was Le Mesnil, we met up with
another airborne group, led by Staff Sergeant Andrews and Sergeant Senier.

Andy Andrews had also had some trouble getting his load out:

I looked at Paddy and said 'Let's get the tail off.' We went inside the
glider and began to undo the nuts holding the tail on, removing them
within a quarter of an hour, but couldn't get the tail to budge! Even
when Paddy jumped on the top it still wouldn't budge! We called the
two drivers over and then began the oddest tug-of-war I ever competed
in. One Horsa Mark I and four tired and sweating airborne types. The
glider won and while we sat back exhausted for a moment, it sat back
contentedly, for all the World as if it was back in England. We thought
of using the charge to blow the tail off, but apart from the noise, and the
fact that we were undisturbed, the type of equipment we were carrying
decided us against it. Then, just as we picked up the handsaw; we heard
the sound of approaching aircraft, and right above us the air seemed full
of parachutes. It was a wonderful sight and we didn't feel lonely any
more. For the next five minutes we were busy dodging kit bags which
dangled from the feet of heavily-loaded paratroopers. One even landed
on the tail, but nothing happened, and when we asked for help to get the
tail off he grinned and vanished. An Albemarle on our left lit up with
flames, which brought us back to earth with a jolt.

There was nothing for it but to saw the tail off. My knuckles were
already sore from the exertions inside the glider, and Paddy, who was

as strong in the arms as anyone I knew, took first shift. We must have been sawing for about forty-five minutes when the driver looking out on the left gave us warning. Silhouetted against the skyline were ten armed men coming towards us. We crouched on the ground and debated whether they were Germans or paratroopers. They moved up to within touching distance and then we heard them speak. They were ours. Thank goodness! The password, 'Punch' and the answer, 'Judy', for the night was exchanged. But would they help us with our tail- Not a bit of it!

They moved on to Ranville, not a bit interested. We had already decided that the only way to get the tail off was to get more man-power. There could be nothing holding the tail on now except sheer willpower! Then the comparative silence was disturbed by the hunting horn, which we had read had been used in the African campaigns, and the paratroopers went in to attack Ranville.

For fifteen minutes there was a great deal of small-arms fire and a house burst into flames about a mile away. The fact that we felt sure that we were on 'British' ground gave us confidence and we decided to make our way towards the village. We crossed the road, Paddy darting across and knocking the compass out of my hand. I had already taken a bearing and we didn't need it any more anyhow. We crossed a small orchard when, in our tracks, and with a very low trajectory, something which I judged to be an anti-tank gun fired twice. We decided that we had best make a detour and went back to the road.

'Punch!' came the challenge. 'Judy' we breathed. It turned out to be two signallers, one of whom had injured his foot in a tree, together with a Canadian major from the R.Es who, screened by the hedge, was trying to pick up his bearings. He had already walked a long way, he said. It turned out he was one of Brigadier Hill's party. I told him where I thought we were and it agreed with his guess. I then suggested that the best plan would be to make for the rendezvous we were supposed to be at for dawn, as we expected by then that Brigadier Hill would be there to set up his H.Q. There were two possible routes. On towards the coast and turn right, or towards Ranville and turn left. We chose the latter, and learned later that it had been the right choice.

The glider hadn't been forgotten, and together our party of seven made our way towards the glider again. It was still standing in glorious dignity. Then the major went up to it and said 'Is this the tail?'—gave two little pushes and the thing fell off! Now the drivers sprang forward, adjusted the steering wheels and we were all ready to go.

Once again our attention was distracted by the drone of aircraft. This time it was Hamilcars and Horsas. One landed not too far away, the others went over the brow of a small rise towards Ranville. We walked over to the glider pilots who were having no trouble unloading. We exchanged names, just in case, then went back to our jeeps, where we met up with Lieutenant Dodwell's party.

The new arrivals were from the third and final wave of *Tonga* gliders, which would put the time at around 0320 hours.

In, or more accurately, below, Chalk 69, Ron Bartley was beginning to come to terms with his predicament:

I whispered 'JB' and got a grunt in reply. However, he was only stunned and the next second we were struggling to free ourselves. My back hurt like the devil! JB passed out the rifles and ammo—which took some finding and extracting from the debris, and then we thought about our two passengers, Harpo and Marx. We called them quietly and got no reply. Considering the state of the glider, with her tail, in which they had both been sitting, perched on top of a tree, we said that they must be dead.

The next second they emerged from the darkness and were immensely relieved to find us alive and kicking. They in turn presumed that we had gone for the usual Burton! We posted one as sentry and set about trying to extract a jeep. The time would now be about 1 a.m. Our own Dakotas and other tugs overhead were dropping bombs that came all too close. (Each of the cargo aircraft were carrying a couple of 250 lb bombs to drop in the general vicinity of the Germans to cause alarm and despondency.) This however, was probably a good thing, as it covered the noise we were making ripping up the glider.

As dawn approached our chances of even salvaging one jeep seemed remote. However, with the driver giving her full throttle and the rest of us pulling and levering, she suddenly shot herself free. The wheels were buckled to blazes, one of them almost horizontal, however she went! That was a lot, but our luck was right out. The orchard, in which we had landed, was situated in a tiny valley which was ringed by sturdy trees. There was no way out for the vehicle. We searched every corner and eventually ran the jeep into some marshy ground, from which it was impossible to extricate her. There was nothing for it but to abandon the hope of saving anything and move out on foot without further delay. We had no idea where we were, although I later discovered that we were in the vicinity of Blonville, some eight miles as the crow flies from our LZ. We moved off through the forest in the hope of contacting some more of our troops, all of us walking like cats on a hot tin roof expecting a tripwire or other booby trap at every step.

I remember telling myself to breathe normally or I'd choke, I was so keyed up. We'd picked up two stray parachutists soon after moving off and nearly blundered straight into a helmeted Jerry sentry right in the middle of the forest—couldn't see what he was guarding though! Somebody said 'Shoot him.' I didn't agree. We drew back and bypassed him on the right. Hell of a lot of noise coming from what we took to be the direction of the beach—probably the battleships softening things up before the main landing begins. We just managed to dodge down while a Jerry platoon passed along a small path in front of us. We seemed to have landed bang in the middle of Jerry activity. We then decided to follow our survivor's training and contact someone local and when we got to the edge of the forest we saw a house not far away.

JB knew some pidgin French and crept forward to make contact. He returned with the news that there was an injured Para officer hiding in the top of the barn and that we were all to join him and plan from there. I led, with the others spaced line astern, across a small field towards the barn. We were spread nicely across the field when machine-guns opened up. I spun round like a top and hit the ground. Picking myself up, I raced to a corner of the barn and when I looked back, all the others were lying spread eagled and still, where they had fallen. A woman opened the back door of the house, about eighty yards away, and calmly emptied a jug or pot onto the ground. Bloody ridiculous! Trap? I don't know and never will. I thought all the lads were dead and made a hell of a sprint back across there, through a hail of bullets, and dived into the forest and under a small bush. I couldn't run another yard as my lungs felt as if they were bursting. I tried to wrap myself round a tree, but couldn't hide the effing rifle! There were Jerries in the wood, shouting and shooting at random. I lay there all day, my back hurting like hell. On checking my kit, I realised why I had spun on being hit. My two large ammunition pouches were in shreds, with segments of the grenades lying in the bottom. The grenades were primed .... am I still alive?

As evening fell I couldn't understand why it was so quiet. I must have been further from the beach than I imagined. My thoughts drifted to the fact that I should have been back in the UK by now, lapping up all the glory, and leaving this kind of lark for the PBI! As I made my way carefully down the valley side I, saw a cave on the other side and spent the night in there.

Ron Bartley spent several days hiding in his cave, living off rations smuggled to him by a young woman from a nearby farm who had spotted him. When the hue and cry had died down a little, he left his den, and made his way to Monsieur Paul Haricot, a fifty-year-old member of the Resistance. Monsieur Haricot had already hidden a number of parachutists in Blonville-Terre, and he introduced Ron to them.

The Frenchman's daughter, Mlle Marcelle Haricot, tried on one occasion to smuggle this group through German lines, but without success. For eighty days, Ron was sheltered by this Resistance group, changing their hiding place each night, until meeting the advancing American army at the Falaise Gap.

Ron was wrong about one thing. Not everyone had been killed in the ambush. Jock Bramah had been hit in the lung and was coughing up blood and went into a coma. The Germans disarmed him and left him lying in the field, certain that he was as good as dead. However, the cold of morning revived him and the glider pilot dragged himself to the Bois Bluche farm in the Chemin du Bois.

The farmer's wife, who had two children, sent for a local nurse, Mlle Marie-Louise Le Franc. Unwilling to risk the lives of her children by hiding the pilot in the farm, the two women hid him under a bridge, before arranging to take him to the house of Monsieur Salesse. Every day the brave nurse visited the house to change the dressings and feed JB. When food became scarce he was sheltered in the café in the square at Lieu Bille:

I stayed in this house without incident from the 9th–14th June. My host brought in another British soldier—a paratrooper—he shared my bedroom on the third floor. During the afternoon of 14 we saw a German Sgt and man with a piece of paper in their hand studying the house from the street— but did not think much about it.

Early in the morning of 15th June the Germans raided the house. My host was held up by some of the raiders, but escaped by shooting his way out when a diversion occurred in the shape of the ceiling coming down. Whilst I was in another room getting the paratrooper's Sten and putting on the magazine the Germans shot the paratrooper and killed him—I got back in time to give the leading German a burst and killed one, wounding the other. One of his comrades pulled the wounded man clear. Another threw a stick grenade into the room. This exploded near me but apart from deafening me did no harm (the explosion brought my host's ceiling down and enabled him to get away from his captors). I groaned as if badly hurt and a German who had been taking cover on the landing came towards me. I let him and another one have a burst. One of them fell downstairs and in the confusion I made my escape dressed only in my shirt (but carrying the Sten and two full magazines), through the window which I smashed. My hand was badly cut but I was able to climb down the side of the house with the aid of two wires—which broke before I hit the ground. I landed unhurt and scrambled up. After chasing over gardens and garden walls I reached the road.

I had seen the floor smoking after the bomb and later from the field saw the house on fire and heard the church-bell fire signal. I had already

been warned that if in trouble I should make for a certain address, and I
succeeded in doing this within the hour. Here I met friends and help and
eventually contacted the British troops in Caen on 9th July.'

Jock Bramah also survived Operation Market Garden only to die in a
climbing accident whilst on leave in Scotland.

In the remains of his Horsa, Ron Hellyer was drifting in and out of
consciousness:

Next time I opened my eyes there was no-one about. Someone
somewhere was moaning and I heard a voice ask for water, and then
again in German for *wasser*. I could still not move my body, but found
that my arms and legs would move. Then I realised what had happened.

Strapped into my seat, I had been thrown, seat and part of the
cockpit floor attached to me, clear through the smashed opening of
the windscreen. The force of the aircraft pivoting to port had done
this. Releasing myself from the tangle of seat and straps and flooring,
I crouched on hands and knees to orientate myself. The main mass
of wreckage, a darker mass in the darkness, appeared to be behind
me and to my left as I looked at it. All was quiet and I realised that
apart from Tommy Turner's explosives I was quite unarmed. I think I
was somewhat concussed, because I suddenly found that I was talking
to myself quite loudly and I also found that I was fairly deaf too. As
things slowly focused and I became more aware of my surroundings,
I could discern a hedgerow and against the lighter background,
several moving objects that suddenly and horribly were recognisable
as the helmets of German soldiers. I hastily hugged mother earth and
cursing the fact that I had no weapons; I wriggled through the dirt and
the stubble to a black mass that I prayed was a thicket of some sort.

Well, Lady Luck deserted HS 129 and its occupants that night, but I
think my personal guardian angel was working overtime on my behalf.
That thicket turned out to be the densest tangle of shrubs this side of the
Amazonian Rain Forest. It took me about an hour to wriggle inside it
with more cuts and scratches than a mad tom cat would have given me
and my heart in my mouth for fear that the Hun soldiery would hear me.
But I made it and spent the rest of the night trying to clean and bandage
a multiplicity of cuts and abrasions and a nasty wound in my forearm,
which later on had to be attended to by a medic.

The following day I found that I had become very deaf again and was
frightened to move around a lot because although I couldn't hear any
noise I made, the Krauts moving around the field most certainly would.
I spent the long, long day sucking the boiled sweets and malted milk

tablets from my escape kit. I saw Jerry carry some bodies from the wreck through a gap in the hedgerow—I don't know for sure how many or who they were.

Owing to my period of deafness, all I heard of the invasion forces was a distant, regular boom, boom from the west, which I think was our naval guns. I do not know for sure, but I think I was the only survivor from the crash. Towards nightfall my hearing improved and when it was dark I cautiously emerged from my hidey hole and armed with four-second detonators but no grenades, a wad of plastique and a length of Cortex, plus my maps from my escape kit, I crept westwards in search of friends. Operation Tonga for Horsa HS 129 and its occupants was over. What a waste of young virile lives—but then that is war.

Ron Hellyer was to be captured before he reached Allied lines and spent the rest of the war in a POW camp.

Driver Fuller was also knocked unconscious. In a later interview he recalled coming round and finding Ian Fyfe pinned down by the jeep. He died ten minutes later. Fuller managed to get out of the wreckage and slid into a nearby ditch. From this vantage point he saw the Germans machine-gun the glider. He did not see Ron Hellyer and so also believed all three men were dead. He managed to evade capture and was picked up by advancing British troops.

Even for Lieutenant Pickwoad, whose glider had landed intact, the unloading process did not go as easily as it should have done:

Now the unloading. In practice it was quite simple. One undid the four locking bolts of the tail section and the whole assembly just dropped down! We pulled and jumped on it, for over half an hour, before it came off. Once unloaded we set off towards the RV and soon came across a few Paras, who we joined up with, as they too, were making for the same wood. There were no signs of the remaining gliders from my flight, although the size of our group kept growing. The head of the column had a number of brushes with Jerries, and wounded and prisoners joined the party.

Aubrey Pickwoad was to meet up with most of his missing pilots the next day.

Laurie Weeden, on LZ 'N' had also lost time due to difficulties with removing the tail:

Eventually it parted company with the fuselage, and the jeep, trailer containing medical supplies, and two motorcycles were unloaded and the four passengers, one of whom was the Brigade Ordnance Warrant Officer took their leave. During the unloading, enemy activity was confined to one light anti-aircraft gun some distance away, firing at the planes involved in the paratroop drop.

Uncertain of our whereabouts, we joined a sizeable party of paratroops and then, in the advance towards a nearby village, we were accompanied by a friendly white horse. No opposition was encountered in the village, but as the column moved out en-route for Escoville, it broke into two parts due to enfilade machine-gun fire. I was just about to emerge from the village, where a friendly cafe owner, Monsieur Dessoules, had offered the troops a crate of beer, when I was surprised to learn from a paratroop sergeant that the officers had all been in the, now departed, front end of the column, and that I was now the senior NCO in the part remaining in the village. I offered the paratroop sergeant the command, on the grounds that this was an infantry, rather than flying, situation, but the sergeant declined the chance of a lifetime on the grounds that the troops were not from his company!

On enquiring at a nearby house I discovered that the village was Herouvillette. Rather than risk using the roads I decided that we should move out across country and after about half a mile we sighted in the moonlight, a large group of troops which fortunately turned out to be British and bound for the same rendezvous. The much-enlarged column now made its way eastwards into the cover of the Bois de Bavent and eventually arrived at the Escoville- Troarn road, where an enemy armoured car was sighted and despatched with a PIAT. Shortly thereafter, somewhere round about lunchtime (not a very good lunch that day) we came across the other members of our flight in an orchard opposite the timber yard, at the bottom of the road leading north to Le Mesnil.

This was not the end of the drama to befall members of 14 Flight. Staff Sergeant Bill England, who had also landed on 'N' had not been able to get the tail off his Horsa. At dawn, he borrowed a motorcycle, with the intention of having another go at removing the offending tail section, and headed back to the LZ. A German patrol emerged from a hedge near Herouvillette and opened fire on the rapidly accelerating pilot. Bill England was shot through the knee and catapulted off the motorbike, to be taken prisoner. Later that day a patrol of British parachutists engaged the Germans who had captured England and freed the wounded pilot, whose wounds were serious enough to prevent him ever returning to regimental duty. The ambulance jeep, which Laurie Weeden's glider had delivered, found its way to the RV at the timber yard and was to play an unexpected role in the tasks allotted to the Royal Engineers.

It was not just the gliders that had been scattered all over that part of Normandy. Commanders from the various parachute units were desperately trying to gather enough men and equipment together to do the jobs they came for. The 8th Parachute Battalion had to capture and destroy three bridges over the River Dives before dawn, which was at 0520 hours.

To do this they needed men, explosives, and the means to get both to the bridges on time. 8th Parachute Battalion, under the command of the brilliant Lieutenant-Colonel Alastair Pearson, consisted of 610 fighting soldiers together with medics, signallers, drivers of the RASC and HQ and two troops of 3 Parachute Squadron, R.E., under the command of Major Tim Roseveare.

Out of these, only 140 parachutists and two gliders landed on or near the dropping zone, so they had to wait until 0400 hours before setting off, in the hope that more stragglers would arrive. 3 Para Sqn R.E.'s War Diary (WO 171 1510 145046), written in the field by Tim Roseveare shortly afterwards, lays the blame for this on several things. Firstly, there was the problem of missing or misplaced beacons and lights on the LZ. Another reason for the wide dispersal of the sticks of parachutists had been the effect of flak on inexperienced pilots. To drop parachutists successfully, the pilot needs to throttle back, apply flap, and fly as slowly and as steadily as possible. Some of the newer pilots had flown too fast and had taken 'violent evasive action' when the flak neared their aircraft. Many of the parachutists, who were standing up ready to jump, had been thrown around the inside of the aircraft, thus leading to the sticks being scattered or dropped in the wrong place.

One of those who had problems exiting the plane was Tony Leake, a young private with 8 Parachute Battalion:

The red warning light for parachuting came on at the side of the doorway and then the green for go, but the plane did not slow down and drop us as it should have done. There was confusion inside the aircraft and it was like a nightmare trying to get out in the darkness. All we could see was the open doorway and Number 2 fell down and had to be helped up, causing even more delay. The man in front of me, Number 15, turned round in the doorway and tried to get back in as he thought he was not hooked-up, which would have been very unlikely, but I pushed him out, hooked-up or not, as we could not afford to waste any more time.

However, he was alright and landed safely. I landed approximately a mile south of our Battalion dropping zone, very lucky to be anywhere near it as some of our men were dropped two miles away.

Tim Roseveare's men managed to collect enough explosives together to be able to destroy, or at least prevent normal use of the bridges. However, they only had six trolleys between them, which were not enough to carry the equipment to the bridges. Laurie Weeden's ambulance jeep and trailer were commandeered by the Major and, with eight men on board, raced through Troarn, which was still occupied by the Germans and blew a twenty-foot gap in the bridge there at 0520 hours, returning at 1200 hours to double the size of the gap. At 0915 hours the road and railway bridges at Bures were blown by Captain Tim Juckes and his troop.

The sappers for LZ 'V' had been similarly scattered, with one stick being spread over a distance of three kilometres between Varaville and Robehomme. Many were dropped in the flooded areas of the Dives valley and lost their equipment, or even their lives. However, by 0440 hours, the bridges at Robehomme and Varaville had both been blown.

Although most of the gliders had not landed in the correct place, this phase of Tonga was a limited success. 3 Parachute Squadron, R.E., managed to carry out all their initial and secondary tasks. The left flank of the invasion beaches was secure for the moment and the widely scattered dropping of parachutists had made the numbers of men on the ground seem far more to the Germans than was actually the case. The major failure was to do with 9th Parachute Battalion which was poised to attack Merville.

Chapter Seven

Seven hundred and fifty men of the 9th Battalion the Parachute Regiment enplaned that night. When the time came to leave the rendezvous for the assault there were only one hundred and fifty and no heavy equipment. Many of those parachutists who were missing had landed in the flooded area of the Dives valley and had drowned before they could remove their heavy equipment. Decades later their bodies were still being discovered. The gliders which should have landed on LZ 'V' had been carrying jeeps and trailers loaded with the bridging sections, three-inch mortars, mine detectors, flame throwers, signallers and wireless sets, sappers and their explosives, By 0250 hours, instead of the planned sixty lengths of Bangalore torpedo, with which they had planned to breach the formidable barbed wire at the Battery, they had only sixteen lengths. Their two doctors had arrived by parachute, but had lost their equipment in the drop, and the medical jeeps were still in the orchard with Ron Bartley's glider. Particularly worrying for Colonel Otway was the fact that he could not illuminate the Battery with parachute flares from the three-inch mortars to pinpoint the site for the three gliders who were to land inside the Battery's defences as the attack commenced.

However, 'failure' was not a word to be found in the vocabulary of a member of the Parachute Regiment, unless of course it referred to the enemy. Terence Otway was faced with only one choice—an all-out assault on the Battery, with the few men he had. Rather than a simultaneous attack through four breaches in the wire, he now had only enough troops available to attack through two gaps, which his recce party had quietly cleared through the minefield, relying on touch alone as the mine detectors had been in the gliders. For a commander who cared as deeply for the lives of his men as he did, it must have been a cruel decision to have to make.

To help the gliders find their way to the Battery it had been planned to set up Eureka beacons and a Holophane 'T' approximately 500 yards south of the fortifications. The gliders themselves had been fitted with 'Rebecca' Mk.III in order to pick up the signals. Chalk 28A, flown by Staff

Sergeant Arnold Baldwin and Sergeant Joe Michie had already seen a lot of service, according to its first pilot:

> The three gliders were very late in arriving and then Major Toler gave us the unbelievable news that a cock-up had occurred. The RAF had fitted-up three gliders with arrestor gear and three more with Rebecca-Eureka gear. So a hunt was on for three more gliders to fit them both to. I can only think that the work was done at different M.U.'s. They arrived the day before take-off—two brand spanking new Horsas and one beat-up old one. The Major did the only fair thing he could do and drew lots. Guess who got the short stick!
>
> On the runway the Parachute Regiment men were waiting to board the gliders. While I was counting them on I noticed that, in addition to his normal kit, was also carrying a spare haversack. I asked one what they contained and he replied, 'Grenades'. As l counted thirty men aboard I thought of all the extra weight contained in those haversacks. Two extra flame-throwers and their fuel were also brought on board and I was convinced that we were grossly overloaded. With just minutes to take-off there was absolutely nothing I could do. No-one in their right mind would dare to tell the officer in command that some of these men must remain behind, or alternatively, they must leave the extra small kits behind.

If the tug is to take-off then the glider must lift into the air first. Arnold Baldwin's glider had problems:

> Flight Sergeant Denis Richards, the tug pilot, slowly rolled forward in his Albemarle taking up the slack in his tow-rope, and we began to trundle forwards. After using the usual amount of runway I pulled back on the stick but there was no response. A little further on I tried again—still no response. Then Denis asked me over the intercom, when I was going to lift off I told him I couldn't get off. A few more yards and then Denis said, with great urgency, that if we didn't lift off we would be going through the hedge at the end of the runway. At that moment she lifted very slowly and we both cleared the hedge. Almost immediately the port wing began to slowly drop. I tried to correct it with aileron but it still continued dropping, so I applied opposite rudder. At first there was no effect, and I feared that, being so near to the ground, the wing-tip might strike so I steadily increased right rudder till it was fully extended and slowly the wing came up again. Then I realised that we would have to make the whole flight with full right rudder.
> I tried to speak to Denis through the intercom, a cable running through the tow-rope, but there was so much noise on the line, possibly caused

by the strain on the tow-rope, that we could not hear each other. Before long my right leg became so painful from pressing on the rudder pedal that I asked Joe to put his foot down. Fortunately, he was a hefty lad with stout legs and he was able to take most of the strain off my right leg. We flew like this for some time in fairly clear conditions, but the effort to keep such an unstable aircraft going was a great strain on both of us and the inability to tell Denis of our problems made matters worse. Then I was horrified to see, dead ahead of us, a monstrous cumulus cloud, quite the largest I had ever seen, and we were heading straight for the middle of it. With the glider wanting to do a slow roll I dare not go through the slip-stream and into the low-tow position, so no 'angle of dangle, and I couldn't ask Denis to go round it.'

The 'Angle of Dangle' would only show the gliders position in relation to the tug when the former was in the low-tow position:

How long we were in that cloud I cannot tell, but it was quite the most frightening experience I ever had. We bounced and bumped around with no idea of our relationship to the tug and a terrible fear that we would go completely out of control any second. After what seemed like ages we emerged from the cumulus and there, right ahead of us and in the right position, I could see the tug. And almost immediately and unbelievably there was a slight jerk and I realised that the tug was pulling away from us. The rope had broken. I felt physically sick. Although we had only been training for this job for about three weeks, all the previous months of training had led me to believe that the end of this flight would mean France and at first 1 couldn't accept the fact that we were off tow and still over England. I slumped in my seat feeling utterly dejected and said to Joe, 'I don't give a f___ what happens now.' When he responded, with a great deal of feeling, 'Well I do and I expect that those fellows in the back do as well,' I came out of my trance and began to think about what to do. The ASI read 140, so I eased back on the stick very gently and had a look around.

There, to my amazement and great relief, I saw a runway's lights just off our starboard wing-tip. Fortunately, I had a great deal of night flying experience and it looked like a normal circuit and landing to me. We were flying cross-wind to the runway and I thought, 'Just continue a bit further on this leg, then a nice turn in down the runway'. However, I had barely commenced the down-wind leg when the runway lights went out. I thought they must be flying ops to France and wanted no strangers coming in. It was now pretty dark, the moon being obscured, but I felt pretty optimistic now about a safe landing. Another look at the ASI still showed 140. I knew that couldn't be right, but I also knew with our overload that we would have a much higher stalling speed than normal, so I did nothing to change the glider's attitude.

Turning across wind when I judged the aerodrome to be a little way behind us, I made my turn and then again, as I believed, into the wind. We now had very little height and I was pretty shaken when I dimly saw the outline of a building on either side of us.' By a very lucky fluke, we passed between two hangers. Then we were bumping along on the grass and I had a similar loss of concentration to that when the tow-rope had broken.

Fortunately, Joe had his wits about him and quickly applied the brake. Even so, we made a long run down the field before stopping. The passengers already knew that their big night was a flop, as their officer had been standing in the doorway when the rope broke, and they were a very disconsolate unit as they disembarked.

Joe and I and the officer made our way back to the control tower where I learned that we had landed at Odiham. The whole nightmare had lasted fifty minutes. Before I had time to ask them why they had switched off the runway lights they asked me why I had landed downwind and there was my answer. We always trained with paraffin flares, obviously visible from any approach, and the only occasion I had encountered the hooded runway lights before had been on one occasion at Hurn. I asked if I could be put through to Commander Glider Pilots and had the unpleasant task of reporting to Colonel Chatterton. He didn't sound too happy!

At day-break Joe and I walked down to inspect the Horsa and even after that awful ride I wasn't prepared for what I saw. We must, at one stage, have been either in front of the tug or diving down steeply below it. The yoke of the rope had sawed through the skin of the mainplane on either side of the fuselage and made one complete coil around it before trailing on the grass some few yards behind the tail. The pitot head, mounted above the cockpit, had been flattened, hence the ASI stuck at 140.

I have cursed my luck many, times over that flight. What should have been the greatest event of my life—had it come off nothing could ever have surpassed it—ended in total failure. But what about the luck of the rope breaking near Odiham! We could never have got away with a forced landing anywhere else! And if the rope, after coiling around the fuselage, had also coiled around the elevator? When at noon we returned by truck to Brize I asked Denis how he had managed. He told me that there were times in the cloud when I pulled his tail down so sharply that he was almost standing on it. It was quite the roughest ride he had ever had.

Even after forty-five years I still feel emotionally disturbed when thinking of it and bitter the way things turned out—not bitterness against any individual but against luck which, in this case, was mostly bad.

While not experiencing the same problems as Arnold Baldwin, Chalk 28, flown by Staff Sergeant Stanley Bone and Sergeant L. Dean, did not have a smooth passage over the Channel. Flying conditions were very bad and their 'Angle of Dangle' was inoperative. Fortunately, the glider pilots were in communication with the tug, whose pilot, Flying Officer Garnett, made every effort to avoid cloud. Part way across the Channel there was a rapid drop in the speed of the combination and the pilots experienced a sluggishness of the controls. The bumpy conditions had released the arrestor parachute and the Albemarle tug, which was underpowered for the job at the best of times, was in severe danger of stalling. Realising what had happened, Sergeant Dean released the rogue chute and the tug regained speed.

The plan had been to release the glider over the coast at 5,000 feet, but when they reached it they found that the cloud base was only 1,000 feet. A quick decision was made by Garnett and Bone and the tug took the glider to the Battery position. Neither the tug crew, nor the two glider pilots, spotted any of the aids which were supposed to guide them to the Battery, the red light, which was to flash the letter 'N' identifying 9th Battalion was not lit, there was no triangle of Holophane lights and 'Rebecca' remained ominously dead. In order to positively' identify the Battery, Flying Officer Garnett circled the site four times, his navigation lights on to allow the glider to keep station in the poor visibility. This was a very brave thing to do, considering the amount of accurate flak that it attracted—in fact the Albemarle was hit several times.

The glider released and landed 200 yards to the west of the Battery, although the crew mistakenly supposed that they were much further away. The area around Merville had been pounded into an almost unrecognisable facsimile of a lunar landscape by the Lancaster bombing raid. When they finally got their bearings, the troops, led by Captain Gordon-Brown, advanced towards the Battery. As they advanced they were met by machine-gun fire and encountered a German patrol. As they were dealing with this they saw the success signal go up from the Battery.

The third glider, Chalk 27, flown by Staff Sergeant Dickie Kerr and Sergeant H. Walker, followed minutes behind. They too had flown through the nasty cumulonimbus cloud over Odiham, but had managed to emerge unscathed, thanks to a fully functioning 'Angle of Dangle'. This passage must have been nightmarish for the parachute soldiers inside, as glider travel was a ticket for airsickness in even fairly mild conditions.

The tug pilot, Flight Lieutenant Thompson, had also agreed to fly the glider to Merville, due to low cloud and poor visibility, and made no less than six runs over the Battery with his wing lights on and flashing his identification light as a signal to 9th Parachute Battalion. Both glider and tug received hits in the heavy flak.

Eventually, a red light, flashing the letter 'A', and a triangle of Holophane lights was seen, and the glider released. Lieutenant Hugh Pond was in command of the troops on the glider:

After crossing the Normandy coast we experienced some ack-ack fire, but for me it was all rather detached. We saw the explosions and dimly heard them as distant taps or knocks on the fuselage and it was not at all frightening, particularly while we were still being towed. After cast-off the noise of the shells was louder and maybe once or twice the glider rocked with near misses, but it was not frightening. It was almost like watching a film.

When the glider had cast-off from the tug, Staff Sergeant Kerr had asked me to keep a look-out for any landmarks I might recognise. I stood up close behind him and carefully looked at the ground, where there was now a lot of activity—tracers, grenade and mortar flashes. At this time the glider was hit and lurched dangerously. I looked back at my platoon and to my horror I saw one man, who was carrying a half-cheese shaped demolition charge on his back, on fire and there was a lot of smoke. However, nothing could be done about it.

I'm pretty certain that we flew over the Battery, which we then recognised. The pilot pulled the glider up and tried to go round again. Whether we succeeded in that, or crashed shortly afterwards, outside the perimeter of the Battery, I don't recall. My recollection is that we scrambled out of the glider through a hole in the fuselage, where the aircraft had broken in two, and then we immediately got involved in a fire-fight with some German troops heading towards the Battery. I can dimly remember the glider pilots fighting alongside us, but no detail. One thing for certain, our attitude towards glider pilots and gliderborne troops changed completely, from one of snooty superiority, to absolute admiration.'

Four of Hugh Pond's men were wounded by flak as the glider descended, two of whom later died from those wounds.

Dickie Kerr thought that he had judged the distance to the Battery just right, but when he deployed the arrestor parachute, to slow the burning Horsa, it caught in the trees and the glider fell fifty yards short into the orchard. The Germans, whom Hugh Pond's men engaged, were a strong group of reinforcements sent to aid the defenders. The intervention of the soldiers from the glider was timely, preventing Otway's tiny attacking force being caught between two fires.

Major Ian Toler:

> Almost everything went wrong that could be imagined, but in spite of this, one glider of the three landed sufficiently close to the object to influence the battle.

The late appearance of the marking lights was caused by the wide dispersal of the 9th Battalion, many of whom had much further to travel than was envisaged to set them up, and when the Eureka did eventually arrive it was found to be damaged. This, compounded by the destruction of a carefully memorised landscape by heavy bombing, made accurate landfall of the gliders unlikely. That, and equipment problems were beyond the control of both the Glider Pilot Regiment and 9th Parachute Battalion. Some books attack Terence Otway's plan for being too complicated to be practical. This is probably an unfair criticism. He was assured in the planning stage that his troops could be and would be delivered to certain places at certain times. His plan of attack was based on this premise and he was let down badly.

The action lasted twenty minutes and after that time he had sixty-five effective soldiers left under his command. The destruction of the Merville Battery was only the first of his tasks. The 9th, now with eighty-five effectives, went on to take the village of Amfreville-Le Plein, garrisoned by a force of five hundred Axis soldiers, mainly Russians with German officers and NCOs. They took half the village on 6 June and cleared the remainder out on the 7th.

While Otway's men had been attacking Merville a further seventy-two gliders, of the third wave of *Tonga*, were inbound.

Chapter Eight

Harwell was a busy aerodrome on the night of 5 June. Shortly after the four gliders carrying the heavy equipment for the 9th Parachute Battalion had taken off, a further twenty-one Horsas were preparing to leave for France. In Chalk 77, towed by Pilot Officer Scott, Staff Sergeant Philip 'Tug' Wilson was carrying personnel and equipment from 6th Airborne's Divisional HQ:

We flew around for an hour over England and then headed for the coast. There was rain and flimsy cloud and as we crossed the coast, the tug turned its lights off. I was flying on the silhouette of the Albemarle when suddenly, the glider veered to port. I put on full right rudder and swung the wheel in the same direction to correct the error. At this time I heard the pilot shout over the telephone 'Cast him off.' Then, 'He's pulling me down!' Once the glider was free of the tug, my efforts to correct the error came into play. The glider turned to starboard and dived. When I recovered from the dive I was at 2000 feet and facing the opposite direction. I saw a pier on the port and forward of me, and headed towards it.

I shouted 'Stand by for ditching' and the troops in the back battered a hole in the top of the glider. As I prepared to ditch, my co-pilot, Sergeant Harris, switched the landing light on. I made three attempts to level out, but on the first two I was miles too high—though the third attempt was just right. We mushed into the water and the cockpit, which was in front of the main bulkhead, just vanished. Both pilots were left hanging by their straps as the glider rocked on its axis. The airlines had fractured and were going 'Schweppes' in front of me. I tried hard to get a mouthful of it, but only got a mouth full of water! I think then that I started to drown as I began to feel slightly boozed. The rocking stopped and I climbed round the side of the glider and began to work my way to the top of the fuselage, kicking through the side in order to get a foot-hold.

While this was going on I could hear someone screaming from inside the glider 'Holy Mary Mother of Jesus Christ—Save me!' The corporal was trapped in the sinking glider by the motorbike, which had broken loose. I gather that a signalman was trying to pull the bike away, but could not move it. On my second kick I struck something solid and at the same instant, the screaming stopped. We all climbed on top of the glider, flashing the light provided, and were prepared to wait until it broke up.

We knew that we were not too far out, for after about half an hour, an elderly chap appeared in a rowing boat and after enquiring about our health, he said 'I cannot take any of you—I'm sinking, but I'll inform the Coastguard."

Flying Officer Geoffrey Lockwood was in command of an RAF Air-Sea Rescue launch, which was stationed in Shoreham Harbour:

Shortly before 0300 hours we received instructions to attend an aircraft which had ditched half a mile away. We left the harbour at full speed and made a square search in good visibility, using searchlight. We found nothing, so continued searching, but changed direction towards Brighton.

At 0310 hours we received another call to tell us that our previous instructions were wrong and the aircraft, a glider in fact, had ditched off Worthing. We made best possible speed towards this new position and located the glider, whose crew were standing on the fuselage. My Medical Orderly administered First Aid, though despite the rough landing, there was nothing more than a few cuts and bruises for him to treat.

The crew of the rescue launch were brimming with excitement as this was their first real rescue. Tug Wilson and his party were returned to Shoreham Harbour. It had not been the old chap in the rowing boat who had alerted the Air Sea Rescue launch, but an aircrew from an RAF rest home, who had seen the glider ditch:

During the night the glider came in on the tide and beached itself. We arrived at the beach at daylight and the signalmen thought that they could get the jeep going, so we could return to Harwell and get another glider for a later lift., We manhandled the jeep, trailer, plus load, as well as the motorbike onto the beach, but nothing would start, so we decided to leave it to be picked up by landing craft.

On asking an ack-ack gunner, who was standing behind the beach, for a hand, he replied, 'Do you think I'm fool enough to come down that mined beach!' He'd only been watching us for an hour! The rope was still attached to the glider and we could see that it had broken at the, splice.

The toe of my boot had a round circle on it—just like the end of a motorbike handlebar! I have often wondered if it was me and not 'Holy Mary' who had unintentionally released the motorbike. One of the signalmen in the back commented that he hadn't even got his feet wet until he had come forward to help the trapped corporal. After we had' dropped off the signalmen, we returned to Fargo Camp, where one of the 'newish' officers tore us off a strip for being a little scruffy!

Also down in the sea was Chalk 99, piloted by Staff Sergeant Ronald New and Sergeant John Gibbons of 'D' Squadron. They had on board a party from 4th Airlanding Anti-Tank Battery led by Lieutenant Samuel Lyons. A few miles off the Normandy coast flak exploded between the glider and its Halifax tug. The tug crew reported that the glider pulled up and overshot them, causing the rope to break, however the account of the sole survivor, Bombardier R. Letherbarrow, gave a different version for the separation:

> It was about 02.45 hrs when we came down in the sea, about 6 miles from the French coast. According to the Glider Pilot a piece of shrapnel had severed the tow rope. Everybody except one Glider Pilot managed to get out of the glider. Gnr. Machin and myself were in the back, the rest were up at the front. We all managed to get on top of the glider, except Bdr. Hill, who when I saw him was 80 yds away, still alive and being kept afloat by his life-belt.
>
> The glider broke up after about ¾ hr. and Gnrs. Taylor and Machin disappeared. Soon after the Glider Pilot was washed off, leaving Mr Lyons and myself clinging to the wreckage (a piece of the tail). About 10 mins. before I was picked up, Mr Lyons was washed away, he went under and I did not see him again. I was picked up at 06.15 approx. by a rescue launch.

The bodies of Ronald New, Samuel Lyons, John Machin and Raymond Taylor all washed up at different points and so they are buried in different cemeteries. The bodies of John Gibbons and John Hill were not found and so the two men are remembered on the Bayeux Memorial.

Not all the gliders whose flights ended abruptly landed in the sea. Chalk 37, from 'B' Squadron, with Staff Sergeant A. Shepherd and Sergeant L. Bullivant at the controls, was forced to return to Brize Norton when they developed aileron control trouble, their glider becoming unmanageable.

Captain B. Murdoch and Sergeant T. Page, in a 'D' Squadron glider, Chalk 101, hit trouble soon after take-off as Murdoch explained:

> As soon as I was airborne I knew that I was in for a hard journey. Glider was grossly overloaded and controls were sloppy. I had to keep picking

up my wings with rudder. I warned my tug pilot to take turns carefully. Later, in avoiding another combination, my tug took violent avoiding action, turning to starboard I followed as best I could but, in order to avoid a collision, had to go down to low-tow position. The port yoke caught over the pitot head. I attempted to free it but got out of position and the rope snapped, taking the pitot-head with it. I force landed near Winchester—no casualties—nose wheel of glider broken. I took the gun and jeep out, realising that I had to get back to Tarrant Rushton at once, in order to get over on the next lift.

This was witnessed by Flying Office Carpenter, whose Halifax was towing Chalk 120. Captain Murdoch and his passengers flew out on the evening of 6th June in a Hamilcar.

Two more gliders from Tarrant Rushton force landed in England that night. Staff Sergeant Bashforth and Sergeant Dray reported that:

... after take-off we had no difficulties, with the exception of a few vicious slipstreams, until 3 to 4 miles N. W. of Chichester when, in a slipstream, the port rope pulled out. Being badly out of position, and unable to rejoin the correct position in spite of determined efforts on the part of both pilots, and with, as a consequence, the tug diving steeply away to starboard I released the other rope. Fortunately, we discovered an aerodrome, but not being given the 'letter of the day' nor the 'colour of the day' could not identify myself, and on asking for recognition with my landing light, the immediate response gained from the 'drome was the switching out of all lights. Having memorised the position of the flare-path I hoped for the best and just made it. The landing was good, no damage or casualties being sustained I was followed about five minutes later by a Hamilcar which, too, force landed.

Bashforth and Dray, too, went over to France on the next day, although they flew their own Horsa. The Hamilcar which force landed at Ford Aerodrome five minutes after them, was one of the Hamilcars from 'C' Squadron. Flown by Staff Sergeant H. Dent and Sergeant D. Rogers, Chalk 502 had broken its tow-rope in the turbulent conditions.

At roughly the same time that the Air Sea Rescue launch was searching for Tug Wilson's glider, Taffy Howe and Bill Shannon were looking for a place to land. Their only reply to the flak, which was continually striking the glider, had been to drop the tow-rope! Bill Shannon helped to control the glider:

By now, she was not very responsive to the controls and turning to port, Taffy said he was going to land on the beach. However, I reminded him of the warning at briefing that the beaches would be mined, and he decided to ditch near the beach, launch the dinghy and join up with the invasion fleet further west. The last height I called was sixty feet, when a shell burst on the canopy. The next thing I knew was fighting my way through the wreckage and cables up to the surface. All trace of the cockpit had disappeared, but the bulkhead doors were still in place, the outer section of the starboard wing was missing and the port wing was partly submerged.

Taffy also surfaced and a heavy rate of machine-gun fire was aimed at us from the shore. I swam round to the starboard side, which was to seaward, intending to climb aboard, but Taffy swam round towards the port wing. Hanging onto 'the tail strut, I was able to remove my boots and anklets and climb aboard.

Most of the fin and rudder was broken away and several large holes appeared in the fuselage. Scrambling forward to the nose, I found that Taffy had disappeared, probably a victim of the machine-gun fire. Four of the signalmen had got out safely, but one, a non-swimmer, was still sitting strapped in his seat, fully equipped—he had not prepared for ditching when warned. Eventually, he was manhandled onto the top of the fuselage, but was in a state of shock and unable to help himself he slid over the edge and never resurfaced.

There was a lull in the firing, but not for too long, for there was a short-circuit and all the aircraft lights came on for a brief period. The firing commenced with a new vigour, including light cannon. I ordered the troops to abandon the aircraft and swim a little way ahead of it, keeping in touch with each other, until the firing should die down again. My Mae West had been torn and was useless, so I kept afloat with the help of a large tea flask which floated by. After about half an hour, the firing died down and we returned to the glider again.

Once on board, I dropped down into the fuselage to stream the J-type dinghy. The water level varied between waist and neck height as the Horsa rolled and pitched in the swell. Opening the passenger door, I threw the dinghy out and pulled the cord to inflate it. Once again the fickle finger of fate intervened and, as the dinghy started to inflate, a wave washed it inside again. It swelled, pinning me against the side of the fuselage, almost smothering me as it burst. There was nothing left now, but to sit it out. When it was light' we could see the-true extent of the damage. The top of the fuselage was level with the water and the starboard wing, to which we clung, rose at an angle of thirty degrees, broken off about half way. The port wing was completely submerged, or broken off, and all the fuselage aft of the trailing edge of the wing was missing.

At 0630 a party of enemy troops was seen descending the steps of the promenade. They cut a zig-zag path through the wire and mine defences to the water's edge and one shouted, 'Kommen Sie hier mit Handen hoch.' I told the troops to check their pockets for documents, throw their fighting knives into the sea and to make their way ashore. One of our captors later told me that they were Ukrainians. From platoon HQ, which was a blockhouse on the promenade, we were taken to the company HQ in the town, which was the seaside resort of Cabourg, and then, with a one to one escort, to the regimental HQ in a large house, some five miles away in Houlgate. Here, we were put to work unloading wounded of both sides at the RAP. Joined by more Airborne POWs, we finished up at HQ, 711 Div, where we were inspected by the Divisional Commander, in his grey leather coat, and photographed by army cameramen.

One of the photographs taken by the Germans was to have a profound effect on the parents of Bill Shannon. They received notice on 26 June that their younger son was missing in action. On 23 July, they were reading their copy of the *Sunday Pictorial* newspaper, whose front page photograph was a shot of captured Airborne soldiers, taken on 6 June, with the heading 'THANKS BOYS, YOU DID A GRAND JOB.' In the midst of this group was a drawn, but intact-looking Bill Shannon. There was great celebration that day at 17 Parkside Drive, Liverpool. The next day, they received official confirmation through the post that he was a POW. However, by then, this information was out of date.

Chapter Nine

The third wave of gliders were all bound for LZ 'N'. Staff Sergeant Johnny Bowen in Chalk 29 had, as his second pilot, Captain John Smellie, the senior officer from 'B' Squadron on *Tonga*, later killed at Arnhem:

We were first away at 0119 hours and I remember that a red flare was fired as we took off. Much later, I learned that this was a signal that half our undercarriage had fallen off. We flew north to begin with, to Southam, and at first there was no-one with us, but then other gliders and tugs arrived and we got into formation, line astern. Crossing the Channel, I saw one German Me 109 fighter and below us, American gliders heading west. These latter were all showing full lights!

Near Le Havre we met anti-aircraft fire and suddenly emerging from cloud we found that we were near the landing zone. Squadron Leader Reggie Trim, our tug pilot, yelled 'Pull off Johnny, we're there.' I released the tow-rope and descended at about 115 mph. Another glider passed me and, as I flew over the triangle of lights and positioned, myself in the lane between the obstructing poles, I saw that the other glider had hit a pole and was blocking my path. I eased back the wheel, but still hit his fuselage as I flew over. This changed my path and one of the poles smashed into the port side of my cockpit, leaving John Smellie with nothing in front of him. As I eased back to land, having lost the other half of my undercarriage, the nose wheel hit a ditch and came up inside the glider. Then we were safely down with no injuries and load intact— the time 0324 hours.

Unloading the glider, we moved towards a defensive position near Ranville. Hearing voices on the other side of the hedge, we decided to give the password. This nearly proved to be our last word, as it was the wrong password! We had been given the one for twelve hours later. Having persuaded them that we were on their side, we continued to our rendezvous and dug in near an orchard. Containers, dropped by parachute, contained pyjamas and whisky!

At about noon, whilst on patrol in the orchard, I received a shrapnel wound to the temple from a mortar bomb. I was evacuated to a chateau which was being used as a first-aid post and was given the Last Rites, not being expected to recover. For several years I had had a premonition that I would not live past thirty-two years of age, and only a few weeks before, I had celebrated my thirty-second birthday. I was convinced that I was going to die and was at peace. I was given a large shot of morphine to help with the pain. It was the high-pitched voice of a doctor which brought me round. I was taken to the beach, where a DUKW was waiting to transfer me to a ship, but on the way to the ship we were strafed by a fighter, and the chap above me was hit. Once again I had escaped death. On arrival in England I was sent to a hospital in Stoke-on-Trent and recovered in time to return to my squadron for Operation Market Garden, the landing at Arnhem.

Another 'B' Squadron pilot was Staff Sergeant George Nye in Chalk 31:

It was approximately 0140 hours when we started to roll. As usual, take-off was smooth and without problems. I checked on the intercom with the tug pilot, Pilot Officer Nichols, before taking up low-tow position. We had good and clear visibility when attaining operational height and were observing aircraft in large numbers returning from the Continent, as they were putting on navigation lights when crossing the English coast – I assumed, for the benefit of aircraft going south. The navigator of the tug informed me we were passing over our landfall, Littlehampton and were on course. The blue trailing lights were, as usual, very helpful in maintaining position and although a clear trip had been suggested at briefing, at no time was the flight free of cloud. In fact on nearing the French coast, the cloud thickened considerably. My tug pilot informed me that we were ten minutes from the LZ and shortly afterwards we were subjected to light ack-ack. Whilst admiring the pretty lights, my second pilot, Alan Smith, spotted the landing torches on the starboard side, at the same time as the tug pilot.

Quickly picking up the lights I told Alan to release and we commenced to descend. Having flown past the lights, Alan shouted out their position as I turned to starboard, maintaining a steady curve until in line with the landing lights. I applied flap, half then full, and with small adjustments landed reasonably smoothly, luckily avoiding contact with the anti-landing poles on either side—expel breath!

Our unloading of jeep and trailer was completed very quickly and, after what seemed only minutes, we moved off as a body towards Ranville, passing through a minefield cleared and taped by the Para Engineers, who had preceded us and positioned the lights on our 'flarepath'. With necessary caution we approached Ranville, the night sounds punctuated by fitful small arms fire. The Glider Pilot RV was in an orchard on the west side of Ranville and on our arrival we found a few GPs, plus a braying donkey. Defensive positions were set up and trenches dug. There was now plenty of small arms fire, but as far as we could see, none of it was aimed specifically at us. As it got lighter the fire increased and we had a few casualties. During the afternoon we had a grandstand view of the main landing—there were gliders everywhere.'

Staff Sergeant Colin Hopgood and Sergeant Daniel Phillips, in Chalk 35, had on board Captain Spencer Daisley, the 13th Parachute Battalion's Quartermaster, his Batman, Lance Corporal John Aldred, Driver Edwards and Signalman Douglas Davis. In addition to the passengers, there was a jeep and trailer and two 350 cc motorcycles. All went well with the flight until the combination made landfall. The towrope broke, possibly from anti-aircraft fire, and the glider crashed killing all but Edwards. He managed to get out of the wreckage and was sheltered by a farmer's family until being captured as he was making his way to Allied lines. The pilots and their passengers are buried next to each other in St Vaast-en-Auge churchyard.

Eight of 'B' Squadron's gliders were carrying Royal Engineers and equipment to clear the LZ for the day's main landing, Operation Mallard, scheduled for late evening. Chalks 41–43 carried bulldozers.

Chalk 41, flown by Staff Sergeant K. 'Taff' Evans and Sergeant Johnny Thompson, also carried a last minute passenger. This was War Correspondent David Woodward of the *Manchester Guardian*. Taff Evans was not surprised when the intercom between the tug and the glider failed:

This was 'situation normal'. On the run-up to the LZ, when flying in the low-tow position, I had to make an emergency release to prevent a mid-air collision with another aircraft, which flew right over the top of our heads. Inevitably this caused the loss of the front of the cockpit, leaving Johnny and me 'out in the cold'. It also resulted in a crash landing amongst the poles alongside a road near to the LZ. I was trying to land on the road by the light of a nearby fire but didn't make it. One pole came into the cockpit, or so it seemed, and miraculously, broke off in front of my face. The stump, however, smashed into my groin and therefore, my lower body and legs were completely useless. No-one else was injured, apart from being shaken up.

We came under immediate enemy fire and the RE lieutenant, in charge of the party of Engineers I was carrying, was badly wounded by a burst of machine-gun fire in the left upper chest and David Woodward suffered shrapnel wounds in the shoulder. When things had quietened down, I told the REs, David and Johnny, to take the road to the left and get to Ranville, where they could join the other Airborne units. I couldn't move, apart from pulling myself around by the elbows, so I remained to take care of the Lieutenant as best I could. Just after dawn, we were picked up by some Paras in a jeep and taken to Ranville. During the day, I was moved to a house which had been converted into a Field Dressing Station. During the German counter-attacks that day we came under fire from a sniper and a German tank. A young Commando next to me was hit again by one of the bullets ricocheting off the walls and shells from the tank set the roof on fire.

Later that day, Johnny Thompson found me in the Dressing Station. He'd had a rough time. First, he'd been shot through the top of his head, the bullet passing between his scalp and his skull! Then he'd collected some mortar fragments in his shoulder. However, in true 'GP' style, he carried on. In fact, after checking on me, he went out hunting snipers with a Para sergeant. Finally, when we were evacuated back to the Sword Beach, for the trip back to England by LS(T), he acted as my 'minder' again. I'm happy to say that after a couple of months treatment in hospital, I recovered from my injuries, but was not able to take part in any further operations.

Chalk 42, flown by Staff Sergeant John Brabham and Sergeant Eric Lightowler, got into difficulty just short of the French coast. Encountering cloud, the tug pilot Flying Officer Bryden attempted to find clear air. Unfortunately, this led to the glider swinging well over to starboard. As Bryden tried to correct, he flew into another patch of cloud. As his aircraft emerged the rope broke broke:

> We were at this time at a height of between 1000 and 1200 feet and about half a mile from the French coast and my gunner reported that he last saw the glider heading in towards land.

Sapper Ronald Howard was one of the five Royal Engineers passengers:

> We came down in the sea...about one mile from the French coast.... The pilot we never saw. The Co-Pilot was wounded and was drowned almost immediately. The rest of us straddled the fuselage. The sea was very rough and the glider broke up completely in five minutes. As each wave came along we had a job to keep together. We missed [Sapper] Powell and [Driver] Gibbons after the first five minutes. Neither of them could swim and they didn't have life jackets. That left three of us clinging to the tailpiece, which went down a few minutes later. We managed to get ashore and, as it was then daylight, 'Jerry' saw us and took us all prisoners.

The bodies of Roydon Powell and Ellis Gibbons were not recovered and they are remembered on the Bayeux Memorial. John Brabham is buried in St Desir Cemetery and Eric Lightowler in Ranville Cemetery.

Staff Sergeant Robert Ashby was in charge of Chalk 43:

We landed without damage. Having, as our first contribution to the Invasion, regaled ourselves with mugs of tea from the enormous vacuum flasks thoughtfully provided, we set to work to get the bulldozer out. The Horsa was of the side-loading type, so we let down the strengthened section of fuselage designed for such purposes, fixed the stanchions underneath to hold it up, and positioned, from it to the ground, the steel U-section troughs, down which the bulldozer was supposed to descend.

Unfortunately it didn't! The Sapper got the bulldozer out of the glider all right and into the ramps, but there it stuck. The caterpillar tracks were a very tight fit and the ramps cannot have been absolutely parallel. If the bulldozer would not go down, neither would it go back up, however hard and often the driver tried. I remember thinking that, having brought it all that way at no little trouble and expense, we could hardly leave the machine suspended in mid-air. Something drastic would be justified. Hailing a jeep which happened to be nearby, I attached ropes from it to the props under the loading platform and had them jerked out from under. That did the trick. The bulldozer crashed to the ground, happily undamaged and the right way up. The Sapper, whose name I never did know, drove it off and within the hour it was working clearing the LZ.

There is another circumstance in which my load was unusual. Almost at the last minute before take-off a paratroop sergeant presented himself and asked to be taken over. He had dislocated his shoulder in training and was unfit to jump, yet he was determined to get into the action with his troop. To tell the truth I forgot about him during the flight, and when he emerged from the back of the glider, far from thanking me for a safe ride, 'Landing was a bit rough' was all he said before disappearing into the dark. I never knew his name either! Bearing in mind how much most paratroopers disliked being carried in gliders, I thought he was a pretty game type.

It is interesting that in the official account of the British First and Sixth Airborne Divisions it says of the bulldozers that: 'both machines were working on the strips within an hour of landing'. Why only two bulldozers and not three? Why 'both' when in reality, that clearly wasn't the case. Although the one carried in Robert Ashby's glider was operational fairly quickly, there was no possibility that Taff Evans' machine was. He was still at the glider several hours after landing and the bulldozer had not been moved!

Another of 'B' Squadron's gliders, Chalk 39, hit a pole on landing. Sadly, the second pilot Sergeant Henry Beveridge, was killed by the impact; the passengers, load and the first pilot, Staff Sergeant B. Goodwin, were not harmed.

Although listed in the Load Allocation List as having carried personnel from 5 Parachute Brigade, Chalk 30 was also carrying Royal Engineers. The second pilot, Sergeant Eddie Raspison, described the flight and subsequent landing:

Norman Jenkins and I had a load in Horsa LF 918 with 'B' Squadron, consisting of four RE paratroopers, a jeep and trailer, loaded with pole demolition charges. We must surely not have been the only ones with a similar load, as seventeen gliders of our squadron were to land nose to tail in a pole-less area prepared by paratroopers, dropping in advance in their accustomed manner.

I understood from those in our load that there was a shortage of airborne RE gliderborne personnel, skilled in the job of shearing poles at ground level and that, much to their consternation, they had been detailed to go in with us. My attempt to convince them that they were far more likely to get down in one piece with us than by parachuting in—a fact of which, I personally, was fully convinced. However, it did nothing to alleviate their misgivings at being transported in our wooden contraption. It is of interest to note that prior to crossing the French coast our Albemarle tug (how their pilots hated these aircraft!) was hit by anti-aircraft fire and its port engine caught fire, which necessitated the feathering of the propeller. The offer to cast off, to give the tug a chance of survival, met with the gutsy reply of 'Hang on—I'll get you there' from the skipper, Flying Officer Mike Brott, a New Zealander. He did get us there and to our gratification, just made it back to the coast, crash landing in a field without any injury to the crew.

Our landing approach to the narrow 'runway', where the poles had been cleared in advance, was normal until we passed over the green direction indication lights, where another glider passed just feet below us, going in the opposite direction! This, at our height of possibly 150 feet, necessitated an immediate decision to turn several degrees to starboard, chancing a collision with the poles to the side of our allotted landing area. We fortunately avoided poles, but were brought to an abrupt stop in a small field, by a haystack up against our port wing. The load and paratroopers, the latter very thankfully, were disembarked without undue difficulty. We never did discover who went the wrong way below us or what indeed happened to them, but did elicit the fact that we were the ones going in the proper direction!

Sergeant John Potts, the second pilot of Chalk 45, was to suffer from the vagaries of the navigator's art:

There is no way that one could crown the trip we made as the smallest ribbon of success. I have only one thing to say about the post-operative briefing report filled in by the crew who towed me, and that is any similarity between their report and mine, is purely coincidental. In fact, I sometimes think that we had been on two different trips!
Round about Southampton there was a marker flashing, which we identified. At mid-Channel we saw the Armada stretched out below us. At three thousand feet, against the backdrop of a partly fluorescent sea, you could see this massive congregation of ships. It was impressive— it was awe-inspiring! It was colossal and the sheer magnitude of this collection of vessels was really amazing. At that moment we were having coffee and Bill was flying the glider. We flew in quarter of an hour shifts, because night flying behind a tug is a very tiring process. I felt that I shared, with the waiting troops down below, a sense of the great theatre of war that we were going to embark upon—the drama of it seemed to envelop everything.

I didn't see any of the mid-Channel markers as I was flying at the time. We couldn't get more than three thousand feet that night and there was heavy, scudding cumulo-stratus at that height. When we did approach the enemy coast ahead, and it was quite discernible, although there was no moon, because you could see the white ridge of the waves breaking against the coast and the change of colour down below. We could also see the ribbon stretching eastwards, which was the River Orne, which was to be our landfall mark so we were very confident.

After the War, I spoke with other crews about their experiences of that night and in the first instance there was a variation in our accounts. They all, without exception, recounted light flak. I'm not terribly certain what their definition of 'light flak' is, but I can assure any reader, that as we crossed the estuary, slightly below our starboard wing on that particular night, the greeting that we obtained was certainly not 'light flak'! It roared up at us, mostly to the front, and a great volume of it was to our port side, so accurate, that at the very beginning we could hear the 'clang' as it penetrated the port side of the fuselage and hit the jeep. The port wing was hit at least once and Bill reported a dull, red glow forming almost straight away. Then one 55mm. came right through the floor of the cabin, passed between us, and exited through the top Perspex. You've heard of the expression that it was so close that you could feel the heat of it? I didn't, because it took, with burn, a large, left-hand section of my face with it!

We followed this obvious river, down on our starboard wing, onwards. Radio communication between us and the tug had disappeared by now and they weren't exactly having an easy passage either. They were attempting a corkscrew-like motion, down to the starboard and up to the port, but the volume of anti-aircraft fire was so intense that it didn't really make any difference which way you went.

As I recall, we should have had about eight minutes flying before we got near to the area that had been selected, but after about ten minutes, and by now Bill was taking timings on his stopwatch, nothing could be seen whatsoever—no indications of lights. There was a pall of blackness hanging under the cloud, which was the residue of the bombings. It was the after-bombing dust that was congregating. We were now down to 2500 feet and nothing could be seen, even though we were in our twelfth minute inland. As we passed one belt of anti-aircraft fire there seemed to be another, just waiting in readiness for us. We saw the tug struck and the next second, we were in free flight. We don't know if the tug cast us off or the rope had been severed, but we were in free flight and could see nothing.

Bill, being on the port side, took the controls and just went straight forward and at about 700-800 feet, there in front of us, was an open expanse. We should have known then that we were in some additional form of trouble, because the field was actually bare. There were no anti-glider poles in it and I can recall, although by now I was searching desperately for a field dressing to try and put on my face, that Bill had turned slightly to starboard and he was going to come round for some sort of a landing when we obviously struck some trees with our undercart, because you could feel the shudder as we went in and by some miracle the glider came to a very sudden, immediate and sharp stop. We certainly needed to, because by this time, the port wing was almost completely on fire from one end to another. We talk about speedy departures from gliders. This must have been an all-time British, European and all comers record, because we were out!

On 12th June, my parents received a document from the War Office which said that 'Military Intelligence 6 have stated, that in a broadcast that they have intercepted, that the Germans had indicated that they have captured a Sergeant John Potts. He had been captured and was wounded in the Le Havre area. Now to the best of my knowledge there was no Airborne operation in the Le Havre area at the Invasion and if you look very closely at the map you will see that the River Seine enters into the sea and then travels eastwards to Paris at that point. It does seem, at least to be a very strong possibility, because after all, the Germans would know where Le Havre was, that we had actually crossed the enemy coast over the estuary of the Seine outside Le Havre.

Whether we had actually landed in the middle of a German army corps, I don't know, but I do know that it was such a big formation that they had a German army photography team on board. They had shot something down, and it was almost a cavalry charge, because, very shortly after our exit from the glider, we could hear them coming. The Germans at night had a habit of making more noise than their tanks, mostly because of the metal container of their gas-mask, situated at the back of their belt, against their uniform. They'd come to capture a bomber crew. I can't actually give you the measurement of their surprise, but the possibility is that they had no knowledge that they were going to be intercepted by rapid fire, and that's exactly what happened! There was a delay, while they obviously regrouped and thought, 'What the Hell's going on here!', and then they started firing.

Now I knew, but possibly no-one else did, that we had struck trees on the way in, and where there are trees, there is concealment, so I made off backwards, giving Bill a shout, towards the trees. They were in fact there, but unfortunately for me, there couldn't have been more than five or six trees and what I thought was concealment, was in fact, no more than a very small copse, This I found in 1982, that as I emerged from the woods, I was being filmed by a German newsreel crew. It appears on the film that I am making an heroic charge towards the enemy. In actual fact I'm diving for a ditch to get cover. Unfortunately, the ditch, although giving momentary defence, wound its way back into the field, so running down the ditch to get myself away from enemy fire, I'm actually making my way back into the centre of it. By this time the Germans must have realised that they had found something that they hadn't anticipated and the small arms fire was now complemented by the use of their mortars.

I must have literally walked into one, because I have vague memories of the flash and the sound, and like a Raymond Chandler thriller, a black hole opened up and I dived in. I can just recall being dragged, by whom I don't know. It was daylight when I returned to consciousness and I was lying on the bench in a small church. There were other British troops in a state similar to myself and some of the opposition as well. Bending over me, trying to take away the dressing that somebody had put on, was a German doctor and an orderly. The doctor, who could speak English, told me that my eyes were alright and that my wounds were a mixture. I think he meant burns and shrapnel. My teeth, jaw and head were aching terribly and at that precise moment the church was strafed and they decided that the pilots, that was Jones and myself, were to be separated from the other prisoners. Before we left, we were put together with some Canadian parachutists and filmed, and I can assure you that the commentary was not at all complimentary!

We were, for some reason, handcuffed and while we waited for dusk before setting out, we were given some bread and coffee, which I didn't touch. It was now that we were given a clue as to where we were when we overheard the name Bolbec. We were either near, or in, Bolbec. It is only recently that I have looked at a French map, and sure enough, Bolbec is eight to ten minutes flying time past Le Havre.

I can recall the journey from the church in the dusk of that particular evening. At around midnight, the truck transporting Bill and me, with no less than eight armed guards to escort us, stopped in the centre of the city of Rouen, right beside the statue to the Maid of Orleans. The main reason for our stoppage, I think, was a call of nature by all concerned. We waited, face against the wall of a shop nearby, with a ring of Schmeissers around us. How I could have escaped I can't for the life of me understand, for I could see but little. Etched on my memory is the sight, above the town, of the gently descending lights of the 'Wanganui' of some Pathfinder Force, accompanied immediately by an air-raid warning, and in a matter of minutes, we could hear the crump of bombs somewhere in the area. Without any further ado, we were hustled unceremoniously back into the truck and out of the town in the quickest possible manner, towards Amiens and deposited in the notorious prison there.

The important part about this whole journey is that Bill and I both agree that we did not cross a bridge. In 1944, as far as I am aware, there was only one bridge across the Seine, to the west of Paris, and that was at Rouen and we were most certainly nowhere near the River Seine on that night.

Amiens Prison was a most awesome place. Jones and I were given the privilege of one of the high-security cells. This was put under constant guard, not only at the door, but also at the barbed wire windows as well. All the while I was there, I should think eight days, I only saw an orderly who put some oil on my face and that was it. Around about the eighth day, the doors opened and we were allowed out for our customary exercise. Waiting for us was a Luftwaffe officer, sergeant and four armed men and we were officially handed over to the custody of the Luftwaffe.

We were very much in the wrong place on the night of our flight, possibly more than fifty miles north of track, and as the Horsa wasn't leading the way, but the Albemarle, then the reason for us being so far off course must have been the tug crew, who mistook the River Seine for the River Orne. If we had been anywhere between the Seine and the Orne, we would have had to cross a bridge to get to Amiens. If we were on course as we flew over Southampton, then we must have made a fifty-mile error in flying fifty miles, which to say the least is very poor airmanship and navigation.

However, there is a positive side to this blunder, and in the intervening years I have speculated on what was the action and activity of the nearest Army Group to where we landed. By four o'clock in the morning there would have been long-ranging reports coming in of airborne landings, centred in the Cherbourg, Ranville and Merville areas. What were they to make of the glider that was down north of the River Seine in the direction of Paris? Did they think that we were the first of many? I can imagine that they spent two or three very watchful nights as the Germans expected the main invasion to come north of Le Havre. I often, with a great deal of puckish humour, think to myself, did they possibly keep a whole army group to the north of the River Seine because of one glider that was shot down and was so far off course? If indeed this is what did happen, then this is one of the great unfortunate paradoxes of World War Two, or any other war for that matter!

Unlike most of the 'B' Squadron gliders, Chalk 38, flown by Staff Sergeant Fred Corry and Staff Sergeant Robin Wright, was carrying twenty-eight troops of the Oxs and Bucks Light Infantry:

Both Robin and myself were ex-REs, so we had been meticulous about checking the weight carried by our passengers. As soon as they had boarded, we got them to sit quietly while we examined their kit—the extra grenades were ditched! Almost as soon as we had started to cross the Channel, the intercom between the tug and ourselves went u/s. Luckily, Robin and the tail gunner in the Albemarle, were both expert Morse readers and communication was maintained by Aldis lamp. As instructed by our Squadron Commander, Major Ian Toler, we flew most of the way in the low-tow position. This allowed us to see the glowing exhaust ports of the tug. Once we were over France we pulled up into the high-tow position. Our own glider wasn't fitted with the 'angle-of-dangle' instrument and station-keeping was extremely difficult in the dark, turbulent conditions. On the way across the Channel, Robin, who had brought along a small torch, spent the time when he wasn't required to use the Aldis lamp, reading from a paperback novel. An ex-public schoolboy and the son of an eye surgeon and society beauty, he was probably the most 'laid back' soldier I had the good fortune to serve with, in nearly seven years in the British Army.

At no time did we see any of the identification lights for the LZ and our tug was forced to estimate our release position. Turning into the wind, we headed down into the almost impenetrable blackness, eyes peeled for some sight of the earth rushing up from the gloom. Visibility was so bad, that I committed what was a possible court-martial offence, and switched on my landing light. There, in the beam of the light, we saw ground and made an extremely hard landing on a school playing field in Ranville. We hit so hard that the nose-wheel assembly came up through the cockpit floor, luckily passing between us. As soon as our Horsa came to a halt in a nose-down attitude, Robin leapt over the nose-wheel and heaved at the door. Amazingly, it shot straight up and the soldiers, who had no need of the available ladder, disembarked in under thirty seconds. We then discarded flying helmets (the pot-like hats of pudding dish shape), sorted through the debris of the cockpit, collected our firearms, ammo pouches and steel hats, then sprang through the fuselage door, to finish in the prone firing position. By this time, the infantrymen had determined where they were, and as in a flash, they jumped from their firing positions and fast disappeared into the darkness.

During the flight and landing I didn't feel scared—we were too busy for that, but two events have stuck in my mind all these years. On 6 June, I was standing on a bank at a small chateau, with Jimmy Nash, a sergeant from our squadron, when a shell burst above us. The shrapnel hit him in the back, passing straight through his body. He was dead before he hit the ground. I was only feet away from him, but escaped entirely.' [The same shell, probably from a mortar bursting in the trees, wounded Johnny Bowen].

The other memory was as we arrived at the beach for embarkation. With true GP élan, we had marched from the interior to the beaches with maroon berets firmly pushed down over the right eye, battle helmets slung on shoulders. Then up comes this RN 'type', a Lieutenant-Commander, tin hat dead square on the top of his head. Can you imagine the contrast? This officer, the Beachmaster, marshalled us into groups to await the landing ships. Nearby, laid on top of some concrete pill-boxes, were piles of our dead. It was quite the most nightmarish sight I have ever seen.

Thankfully, most of the tugs delivered their gliders to the proper release point. Out of the seventeen 'B' Squadron gliders despatched for LZ 'N', thirteen of them landed on, or very close to, the LZ. Six of the thirty-four pilots were killed on the operation. 'A' Squadron, who sent twenty-one gliders of the third wave to LZ 'N', had very similar results. Fifteen of them landed successfully on the LZ, six of the pilots being killed in action. Captain Bob Cross, who skippered Chalk 72 with Sergeant C. Bishop witnessed the death of Sergeant Alex Rigg:

One glider had stopped somewhat short on the landing area. A few minutes earlier I had managed to avoid it, having just enough speed to hop over it. Sergeant Rigg's glider struck this other one and overturned, killing him.

Staff Sergeants Ken Kirkham and John Smeaton had been flying partners since their days at Tilshead and were now the crew of Chalk 86. Ken Kirkham was a week short of his nineteenth birthday:

We took off from Harwell at about 01.30, in moonlight obscured by extensive cloud layers, laden with a jeep, a trailer packed with ammunition, a couple of motor cycles, and six men from Divisional Headquarters. We'd hardly settled into the high tow, holding station on the Albemarle tug's blue tail-light and flaring engine exhausts, when over the intercom we heard the navigator's unemotional voice advising skipper Butch Marshall that the 'G' equipment had "gone for a Burton". We were without radio-signal navigational aid. Dead-reckoning in darkness no doubt contributed to our drifting east of the main stream. I can't recall glimpsing another combination during the flight.

Crossing the South Coast, I thought conditions in the Channel looked rough, with white-caps showing briefly in the darkness as far as I could see, before it dawned that, in fact, the white flecks were the bow-waves of the Invasion Fleet ploughing on for France. In the distance, tracer-shells arced in seemingly slow display, but as we neared the French coast heading blindly towards Le Havre, the shells came at us like rockets, flashing lightning-brilliance into the cabin. All at once I became fully aware of the Horsa's plywood skin. Butch stood the Albemarle on its starboard wing-tip in the steepest steep-turn I'd ever seen; we strained to keep the lumbering glider held on a following course, eyes locked on that tail-light. We pulled away from Le Havre's hornet's nest, following the coast dimly seen through cloud shadows, until the mouth of the Orne showed a welcome gleam to port.

We turned inland, and soon spotted Pathfinder beacons faint in the distance, marking Landing Zone 'N'. We cast off; set full flap, and thudded into a French stubble-field, undercarriage, intact; pulled on the brakes, and slewed to a halt in what seemed impenetrable blackness beyond the lamps.

John and I swapped flying helmets for tin-hats, grabbed our rifles, and leaped out to take up defensive watch while the passengers set about unloading. The tail unit was unbolted and steel channels run out in smart order, but the jeep's wheels locked solid, tangled in an abandoned parachute, before the trailer had cleared the channels. Cutting it free cost about 30 minutes of sweated muttered cursing, the surrounding darkness filled with the sounds of sporadic firing, muffled explosions, and the thuds, rumblings, and splintering crashes of other gliders coming in to land. Miraculously, we remained unscathed.

There was a moment when all noise seemed to fade away before erupting again in a spine-chilling burst of wild cheering, rapid firing and the crack of grenades as somewhere near, to the West, some of our lads went into an attack.

The glider of Staff Sergeant Alan 'Yorkie' Stear and Sergeant J. E. 'Eric' Wilson also met with heavy flak as it emerged from cloud near Le Havre. Eric Wilson believes that the evasive action, which the tug took, meant that their approach to the LZ was less than ideal:

The LZ was barely visible through low cloud and smoke and the only illumination to the area was provided by the tracer element of the vicious and persistent 20mm and light ack-ack fire. Just how badly we were positioned became apparent, seconds after Yorkie had cast off from the tug, and as we made our approach. I simultaneously observed on the right hand side of our Horsa, a church spire, which appeared to tower away into infinity in the darkness and on the left hand side, I have visions of seeing, at the same level as myself, a clock face on the wall of a building.

At that instant, we landed and subconsciously congratulated ourselves on having made it when, to my horror, out of the darkness appeared a white building, into which we crashed at eighty or ninety miles an hour. I can vaguely remember one or more of our passengers coming forward to render assistance, but I lost consciousness almost immediately and was to learn later that Yorkie had died instantly. I was trapped in the wreckage for two and a half days and sustained two broken legs. One, being beyond repair, was amputated at the Aid Post in Ranville church.

Staff Sergeant J. Edwards, also of 'A' Squadron, was one of a group of glider pilots who, along with Padre Pare, of 1 Wing GPR, searched the crashed gliders in and around the LZ soon after the naval bombardment had ended:

The first glider we visited had crashed head-on into a brick building. The tail of the Horsa glider had been released, which suggested that a jeep, or some other heavy equipment, had been unloaded. The two pilots were still in the cockpit, both dead. There were about six men, I can't remember the exact number, sitting in the front portion of the glider and all were dead. Yorkie Stear was the first pilot.

The glider had, in fact, hit a small house attached to a cafe and bar, now called the '6 June 44 Estaminet'. The house itself has since been demolished but the cafe, sited at the crossroads in Ranville, still does thriving business. The crash was witnessed by a member of 13th Parachute Battalion, Robert Falkingham, known as 'Black Bob' to his friends. Black Bob, now sadly deceased, was in a slit trench less than thirty yards from the bar. He and his platoon had been given the job of clearing the anti-invasion poles from the Ranville end of the LZ. Three of his platoon, Privates Smith, MacMillan and Brown helped to get the bodies out of the glider. It was then that Eric Wilson probably had his closest brush with death. The bodies of Yorkie Stear and he were laid out and prepared for burial. All present believed that both men were dead, but for some reason, Padre Pare must have had doubts, and held a mirror to Eric's mouth, the faint misting which resulted, showed that they had been about to bury the Glider Pilot alive and he was rushed to the dressing station.

Two of 'A' Squadron's gliders landed in the grounds of the Château de Grangues, five miles to the east of Varaville. The first of these, Chalk 74, was piloted by Staff Sergeant Duncan Wright and Sergeant Barry Powell. On board was a party of Divisional HQ Signallers led by Captain John H. Max, who was attached from 5th Parachute Brigade. Corporal MacDonald was one of those Signallers:

We were hit by flak and shot down and crashed in a field. I do not remember much of the crash as I was hit by flak which took one of my feet off and when I regained consciousness I was lying on a road about five yards from the glider. All I could see was the remains of the glider and Capt. Max staggering around it. He then collapsed onto a wing and fell to the ground. I didn't see him move again. (Sadly, John Max had died of his injuries) Around about 07.00 hours I was captured by 8 German Infantry, who robbed me and then went over to the glider.

[Lance Corporal] Ainsley, [Signalman] Martin and [Lance Corporal] Ellis had minor wounds and went to a Stalag around the 25th June. [Signalman] Howarth and I were prisoners in a hospital in Paris until recaptured by the Americans on the 27th August. I enquired from Howarth about (the pilots) and he said they were both lying crushed and dead under the glider. [Barry Powell was killed but Duncan Wright was taken prisoner].

Chalk 86, half a mile to the east, had also come down hard. Staff Sergeant Roy Luff and Lieutenant John Bromley had on board a Forward Observation Unit led by Captain Robert Hunter. The glider had crashed into the trees and eight of the fourteen men on board had been killed, including both pilots and the youngest passenger, eighteen-year-old naval telegraphist Spencer Porter.

The Château had recently been commandeered by a German army unit for use as a headquarters and the soldiers camped in the grounds quickly captured any Allied personnel unfortunate enough to land there.

Two Stirlings carrying parachutists crashed into the grounds killing thirty-two, injuring four and resulting in the capture of a further eleven who were incarcerated in the stable block with Staff Sergeant Wright. During the night the Germans bound the senior officer, Lieutenant John Shiner, and took him away to another headquarters for interrogation, leaving the glider pilot as senior NCO. The full truth of what happened next will never be known.

A Red Cross worker, Therese Anne, who was sheltering in the cellar with the De Noblet family, the owners of the Château, was called outside by the Germans in the morning. She was asked to make a note of the identification details of eight Allied soldiers who had just been lined up against a wall and shot. The dead included Duncan Wright.

The Germans seemed keen to justify their actions to the French woman and claimed that the soldiers had injured one of the guards in an abortive escape attempt and that was why they had been executed. With a heavy heart, she went about her task collecting identification discs and writing the details in her notebook before going on to record the details of the numerous Allied dead in the other parts of the Château's grounds.

It is probable that there had indeed been an escape attempt. Certainly, the pilots had been instructed that it was their duty to escape if captured and it would have been in character for eight highly motivated Airborne soldiers to try and capitalise on the confusion of that night. However, seventy years on, the penalty paid by them seems a severe one considering the guard was only injured and that it was meted out hours after the alleged escape attempt had taken place.

Staff Sergeant Alan Hunter and Sergeant C. Collins were piloting Chalk 84. On board were a jeep, trailer and a party of Royal Engineers led by Captain Maynard. The glider was being towed by an Albemarle of 570 Squadron piloted by Flying Officer Fisher. His rear gunner was Flying Officer Rascheed RAAF. In their interrogation of the fate of the glider, they reported:

> When over CABOURG at 1600' they emerged from cloud, the glider was badly out of position. The glider regained position and F/O Rascheed saw it hit by flak. Large pieces fell off the glider and it 'fell out of the sky', snapping the tow rope. F/O Rascheed saw it going down for about 300 feet before it disappeared. It was not known which pieces flew off the glider but F/O Rascheed later stated they were either large pieces of the port wing or the tail plane.

The glider made it to land and all on board survived. They were all taken prisoner.

The commander of Force 'Ian' on LZ 'W' was Lieutenant-Colonel Iain Murray, Officer Commanding No. 1 Wing the Glider Pilot Regiment. He

was the senior officer of the Regiment to land in Normandy and flew his
Horsa into LZ 'N' with the 'A' Squadron gliders around 0320 hours:

> My own glider carried a full complement, including Brigadier the Hon.
> Hugh Kindersley, Commanding 6th Airlanding Brigade, some of his staff
> and the war correspondent Chester Wilmot, who was doing a running
> commentary into a recording machine.
> Turning in from the coast, the visibility became very poor. A combination
> of cloud, and the dust and smoke caused by bombing, obscured the
> ground completely. This may have been a godsend as the A.A. fire,
> although considerable, seemed very inaccurate. Nearing our objective
> the visibility improved and soon the flares, put out by the Independent
> Parachute Company, could be seen and gliders cast off from their tugs.
> We managed to make a good landing with plenty of speed so as to take
> avoiding action with the posts. In the last few yards one post tore a wing
> tip and one collapsed when hit head-on by the cockpit. I always think
> that this one must have been loosely placed by some patriotic Frenchman
> employed by the Germans.
> Soon after landing I found that Chester Wilmot's recorder had been
> smashed by a piece of shell from an A.A. gun, which was most unfortunate.
> However, he had a good picture in his mind and his description, which as
> later published in his great book, Struggle for Europe, gave a very clear
> picture of events leading up to the time of landing.' [Chester Wilmot was
> tragically killed in January 1954, when the BOAC Comet that he was a
> passenger in, disintegrated in mid-air over the Mediterranean Sea].

One glider which did fail to make the LZ was that of Major John Royle,
commander of Force 'John', and Lieutenant Smith. Their tow-rope broke
over the coast from the combined stresses of cloud and the flak, the glider
landing heavily in a minefield four miles to the east of the LZ.

They were less than a quarter of a mile from a flak battery and had
in fact severed its telephone lines with the port wing of the glider on the
approach. However, only Lieutenant-Colonel Bray, one of the passengers,
was injured, suffering concussion. The glider was severely damaged and
it was not possible to remove the load—because of this and the close
proximity of the Germans, who were now reacting aggressively to their
intrusion. Major Royle's party fought its way to LZ 'N', luckily without
incurring casualties, with the exception of the unfortunate Lt-Col. Bray,
who was further injured falling off a wall.

Between them, the two squadrons achieved a 74 per cent success rate for
delivering gliders onto the LZ—an outstanding achievement considering
the circumstances.

Chapter Ten

Sergeant R. 'Jock' Simpson, 'C' Squadron, was surprised when he was called to the Squadron Office on the morning of 5 June and told that he was on Operation *Tonga*. Lieutenant Taylorson's second pilot had reported sick and Jock had been selected to take his place in Chalk 500:

A short time after midnight we rolled down the runway and took off, heading towards the Channel and wondering what lay in store for us. The atmosphere in the glider was electric as our passengers the gun crew, were rather excited as they were unable to see anything and consequently, kept calling on the radio telephone until Tommy Taylorson got mad, told them to 'shut up' and said that he would keep them informed when anything transpired.

As we crossed the Channel, tense but calm, we could see the white wakes of the ships of the sea-borne forces as they made their way across the water. The flight was uneventful until we approached the French coast, where we encountered medium and light anti-aircraft fire coming from Le Havre. Fortunately, we escaped being hit, but our Canadian tug pilot, Flying Officer Baird, was hit by a bullet between the toes. Some strong adjectives were heard over the radio telephone, but he carried on and did not falter in his duty.

We proceeded inland, until the tug pilot pointed out the crossroads in front of us, and gave instructions for us to cast off at that point and then to turn right and make a normal approach and landing. At this stage things became very serious as we realised that it was the point of no return and in all honesty, one must admit to having some degree of fear and apprehension.

As we approached for the landing we could see that the area was obstructed by masses of poles standing in the ground and obviously placed there by the Germans as landing obstacles. However, we were very relieved when we realised that our wings were too high, seventeen feet above the ground, to be affected, but unfortunately that was not the case for the Horsas landing in the same area, as their wings were below the height of the poles—consequently they sustained severe damage.

After we rolled to a stop we got out, opened the nose door and released the valves on the landing legs, allowing the Hamilcar to settle on the skids. When the load was released the tractor pulled the gun and ammunition down the ramps. We looked around to see if any of the other Hamilcars were near, but found only the one. This glider had suffered severe damage to the undercarriage, making it impossible for the gun crew to get their equipment through the nose door. Therefore, instead of us going with our own gun, Lieutenant Taylorson and I assisted Staff Sergeant England and Sergeant Hill to cut through their fuselage at the tail end. This proved a considerable task, but with the help of other men, we managed to tow the load through the tail section as daylight was breaking.

After having a bite to eat we decided that we could best assist the expected squadron, who were to arrive later that day loaded with Tetrarch tanks, by laying out a large directional arrow made up of parachutes. This took up a fair bit of time, but shortly after this we observed that the sky was filled with tugs and gliders. As Horsas and Hamilcars approached the landing zone, the Germans opened up with mortar fire, creating havoc whilst the gliders were landing. After unloading, some of the Tetrarch tanks made a concerted attack and disposed of the mortars.

The first figure whom we recognised was Major Dickie Dale, our Squadron Commander, who nonchalantly walked across the landing zone wearing his red beret instead of his helmet, which at that time contained a large bottle of whisky. The mortars had created quite a bit of damage to the gliders, and unfortunately we found that one of our pilots had been quite seriously wounded when a mortar bomb had exploded at his feet. Sergeant Hill and I volunteered to stay with him until the medics arrived to take over. He was in extreme pain and whilst with him we administered two injections of morphine, which we were supplied with before any operation. The medics were too late as he died in our arms.

After this, we proceeded to join the Squadron where they had taken up position. By this time, Sergeant Hill and myself were feeling rather cold and dejected, but Major Dale seeing our plight, poured out some of his whisky for us before we moved into our defensive position. Needless to say, the whisky was gratefully received.

Chalk 501, nicknamed the *Bag of Bagdad* and flown by Staff Sergeant Leslie Ridings and Sergeant Ronald Harris, ran into trouble shortly before the LZ. The combination had had the unusual experience, four minutes

1 S/Sgts Johnny Bowen and 'Lofty' Lawrence. (*Johnny Bowen*)

2 S/Sgt Billy Marfleet. (*Stephen Wright*)

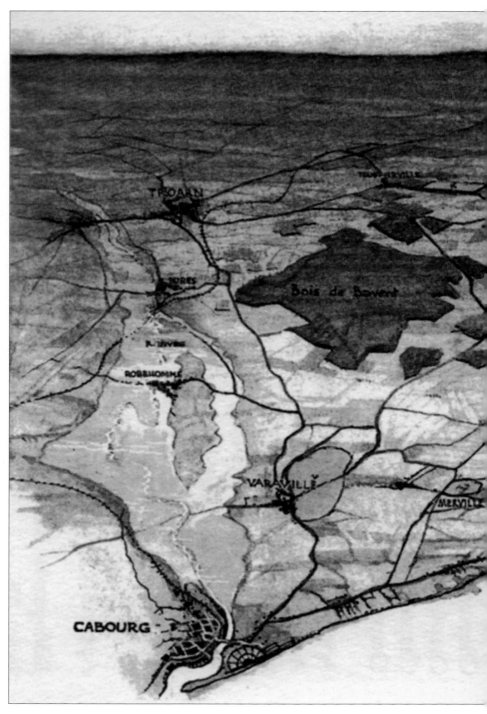

3 Tonga map.

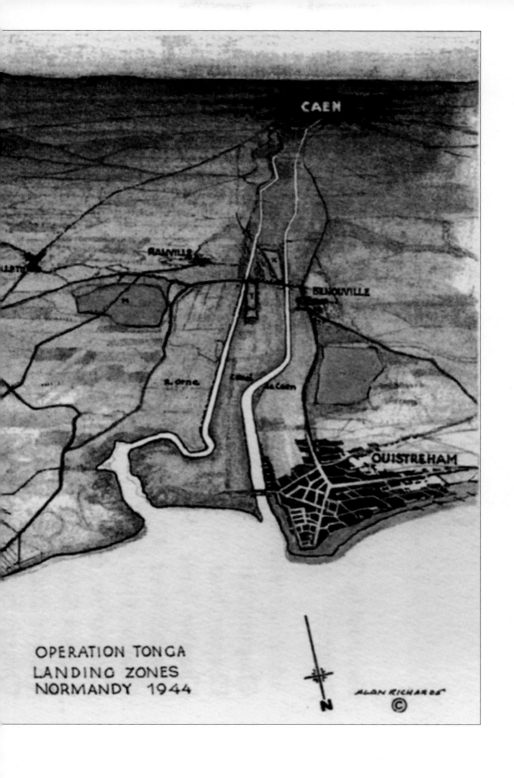

CAEN

RAUVILLE

BENOUVILLE

R. Orne

Canal

R. Caen

OUISTREHAM

OPERATION TONGA
LANDING ZONES
NORMANDY 1944

N

ALAN RICHARDS ©

4 Some of the Tonga pilots in basic flight training at Stoke Orchard: Back (left to right): ?, Jenkins, Sampson, Nash, Startup, , ?.?, ?; Middle: Bowen, ?, ?, ?; Front: Raspison, ?, ?, Harris (*Johnny Bowen*)

5 5 June 1944: Final briefing at Brize Norton. Second left: Sqn Ldr Reggie Trim; Right: S/Sgt Johnny Bowen; Foreground: Capt. John Smellie. (*Johnny Bowen*)

6 Loading trials pre D-Day. S/Sgt Johnny Bowen at the top of the ramp. (*Johnny Bowen*)

7 Left to right: Bruce Hobbs DFM, Stan Pearson DFM, Bill Herbert DFM, Jim Wallwork DFM, Tommy Moore MM, outside Buckingham Palace on 1 December 1944. (*Eagle Magazine*)

8 Bill Ridgeway after capture (far right). Note that the German guard with the 'Iron Cross' is carrying a Sten. (*Eagle Magazine*)

9 Temporary grave of Sgt Dick Chadwick (*Diana Bailey, neé Chadwick*)

10 Air reconnaissance photo carried by Andy Andrews. The white circle on the left is the Merville Battery. The two areas outlined in white, on the right, are the two parts of LZ 'V'. (*Andy Andrews*)

11 Map of area, complete with folds and sweat stains, carried by Andy Andrews on 'Tonga'. (*Andy Andrews*)

12 'Passport' photos carried by members of 'E' Squadron to aid production of counterfeit civilian ID cards. (*Andy Andrews*)

13 Front page photo from *Sunday Pictorial*, 23 July 1944. Sgt Bill Shannon fourth from right. (*Kevin Shannon*)

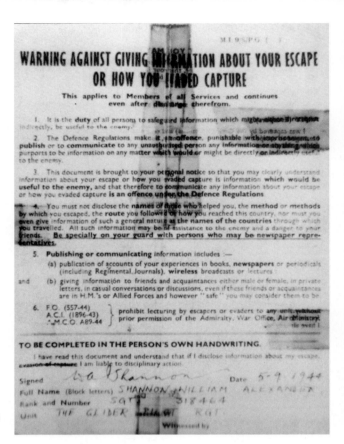

14 MI9 form which
successful escapers had to
sign. (*Kevin Shannon*)

15 View of Halifax from Horsa in 'high tow' position. (*Kevin Shannon*)

16 Horsa landing. Note steep angle of approach and barn door-like flaps. (*Kevin Shannon*)

17 A different angle. (*Kevin Shannon*)

18 A good view of the enormous flaps. (*Kevin Shannon*)

19 Last few feet.
(*Kevin Shannon*)

20 LZ 'N' on
6 June 1944.
The Hamilcar to
right of picture
is Chalk 500,
flown by Lt
Taylorson and
Sgt Simpson.
(*'Jock' Simpson*)

21 The café at Lieu Bille from which 'Jock' Bramah made his daring escape. (*Stephen Wright*)

22 The pilots disguised as Polish workers at the farm of Jean Deguerne with members of the family. (*Kevin Shannon*)

23 The Herbé family outside the shop. (*Kevin Shannon*)

24 The Herbé's shop after
the rainstorm. (*Kevin
Shannon*)

25 Bryan Helme, Sandy Dow, two U.S. airmen, Bill Shannon with Madame Herbé and her daughters on Liberation Day. (*Kevin Shannon*)

26 Bryan Helme, the Herbé Family and Adam Hunt, (*Kevin Shannon*)

27 Assault Groupe 'Bourlon' on Liberation Day. (*Kevin Shannon*)

28 Assault Groupe 'Bourlon' with a tank retaken from the Germans on Liberation Day. (*Kevin Shannon*)

29 Survivors of Groupe 'Bourlon' celebrate the thirtieth anniversary of Liberation. (*Kevin Shannon*)

30 Glider pilots at 1968 Reunion. Left to right: John Potts, Bill Shannon, Bill Higgs, ?, Harry Gibbons, Len Afolter. (*Kevin Shannon*)

31 Graves in St Vaast-en-Auge Churchyard: Capt. Spencer Daisley (far left), Signalman Douglas Davis, S/Sgt Les Ridings, Gnr Frank Newham and Bdr William Whitney (far right). (*Stephen Wright*)

before reaching the coast, of a parachute floating down past the Halifax and hitting the starboard wing of the glider, although no damage was caused. Flying Officer Sizmur, the captain of the towing Halifax, reported that the tow-rope broke at 0327 hours, two minutes after they had crossed the coast. He thought that the Hamilcar may have actually landed on the LZ. Sadly, he was wrong.

The Hamilcar landed in an orchard near the village of St Vaast-en-Auge. At dawn, the Germans attacked the glider, killing three of the gunners from 3 Airlanding Anti-Tank Battery: Bombardier William Whitney, and Gunners Frank Newham and Douglas Stanley. Staff Sergeant Ridings was mortally wounded and died the next day. However, Sergeant Harris managed to escape and joined up with a sergeant major and a sergeant from the 1st Canadian Parachute Battalion, who had been dropped eight miles from their DZ.

The three men managed, without the help of the local population, to evade capture for ten days before being caught by the Germans near Pont l'Évêque.

Sharing Tarrant Rushton airfield with 'C' Squadron had been the thirty gliders of 'D' Squadron. These were to deliver the six-pounder anti-tank guns of 4th Airlanding Anti-Tank Battery and FOO Teams from Divisional HQ and 3rd Parachute Brigade. Staff Sergeant Ernie Stocker, the first pilot of Chalk 121, made the flight in severe discomfort, with six boils on his backside:

I can remember that in the briefing we were told that we would see flak from Le Havre on our port side, the 'twin water ribbons' and that there would be indicator lights in the area. It seemed to me, that when we got there, the flak was not to port, but almost from below and we saw neither lights nor the 'twin waters'!

After a while my tug pilot, Flight Sergeant Griffiths, said 'You'll have to go, Ernie—my fuel is running low. See you back in the Mess.' So we pulled off and almost immediately saw the 'twin waters' and pursued the normal approach and landing technique.

It is my belief that the wind direction was not in keeping with that given at briefing and in fact, I have good reason to believe that it was almost in the opposite direction! My good reason was my ground speed on landing. It is common practice today to have 'assisted braking'. That night, my 'assisted braking' was by means of two anti-invasion poles, nicely placed, one on each wing, By the way, I had prayed on the way down! A mate of mine, who cannot be named, broke all the rules by switching on his landing light. l didn't think of it—too busy praying I guess!

With reference to our rough landing. We were carrying a party of Forward Signals, commanded by a Lieutenant Leicester. l remember him well! One of the responsibilities of the glider pilot was to make sure that all equipment was secure and that all personnel were properly harnessed. We did that and I said 'Remember—everybody stays harnessed until instructed by me or my second pilot, Sgt Allan.' 'O.K.' they said. As is known when you 'pull off', there is a pronounced bump.

Lieutenant Leicester decided we had landed and unbelted. Then we had the 'abrupt' landing! The cockpit then contained us two, Ernie and Stan, plus the helmeted head of Lieutenant Leicester, who had arrived by crashing his way head first through the ply door. He survived it, but was badly shaken and getting him free delayed our unloading somewhat, so that it was getting daylight by the time we had finished. I'm sure the Lieutenant was still seeing stars! The unloading had been achieved in text book fashion by the efficient Signals Sergeant.

They didn't want us! So Stan and I moved towards Ranville and en route, bumped into a major with some POW's. 'Take care of this bunch' he said, which of course we did. We found a safe place down the road embankment with our six prisoners and one 'suspect' Frenchman. They didn't seem aggressive in any way- they appeared afraid. After all, they had been turfed out of bed in the small hours! We were then joined by another glider pilot, who had misplaced his first pilot, so our guard duties were eased.

Sometime later in the day, walking along the road which was some ten feet elevated and right on the skyline, came this six-foot four-inch tall man, with no helmet on and a shock of white hair. Walking with him was his corporal bodyguard with a Sten and that's all! It was General Gale—known of course, right from his schooldays at Rossall, as 'Windy'. He looked fearless while we were cringing! He said to me, 'Where's the enemy?' It should be remembered that the whole situation was fluid and firing was taking place in all different directions, so l said 'I don't know, Sir.' He said 'Come on, Corporal. Let's find somebody who does know something about this bloody war!' It's little wonder that he figures so high on Rossall's honours board!

We had no provisions, apart from that granite chocolate, and were desperate for a drink and so were our POW's, so l decided to scout around for some water and (heaven) some tea. I saw a soldier in a spinney. He was brewing up—I could tell that, even from a distance of some thirty yards, so l started towards him. A mortar crumped and we both hit the deck. After a while I got up—he didn't! He was dead, although I couldn't see a mark on him, and his brewing equipment had disappeared. I found some of his unit, the South Staffs, about three hundred yards away and handed the problem over to them.

Later that evening, or it may have been the next—my memory is a bit uncertain here—we were relieved by members of the 41st. We were absolutely exhausted and I found a farm and a farmyard where there was a large midden. I fell on that and fell asleep, I would think, for about ten hours. Strange thing is that no-one disturbed me. I don't know where Stan and the other GP went.

When I awoke, I had to make my way, the six miles or so, to the beach and report to the Beachmaster, to hitch a lift back home, which I did, but desperate for a cup of tea. On the way I saw a couple of soldiers brewing up at the side of a haystack and joined them with a begging expression on my face. The water was almost on the boil when this plane started dropping its bombs.

We studied the course of the bombs and decided that t'other side of the haystack was safer and scarpered. When the attack was over, we returned to our brew, but it had all disappeared—in its place was a big hole!

I moved on to the coast and found the Beachmaster. At first he was friendly, but then suddenly backed off some ten feet. He said 'God! You stink. You'd better be careful, otherwise you'll be raped by a polecat!' Wading to board the landing craft helped to remove some of the stink, but not a lot. The boat crew kept well downwind of me until we landed at Newhaven. I'd like to think that my smell and the sticky backside was due to either my six boils bursting or my kip in the midden, not surely the third possible cause!

Bill Musitano, in Chalk 119, was carrying a six-pounder anti-tank gun in his glider:

As we approached the coast of France, in Horsa PF 803, we saw the flak come up. Much of it was tracer and as we flew on at 160 mph, it passed us by in fast moving streaks. It was now that we discovered a major problem. The wind had been forecast as blowing from south to north, but was in fact blowing in almost the opposite direction. The green 'T' was only visible from the air when approaching into the wind. These had been laid out 'as briefed', but we were approaching into wind. As the 'T' was not visible we had to rely on the navigator of the Halifax to tell us when to release. He was good, but maybe thirty or sixty seconds out. I remember he said 'Now' and I pulled the 'tit' and we were free. A gentle turn to starboard showed us the 'T' and I believe I said to Paddy 'It's too far away!'

With our full load, the vital seconds delay in pulling off, meant that we were going to land about half a mile short of the LZ. I put on half flap to get maximum gliding distance and we waited. We were gliding at around seventy, perhaps ten above stalling point, when up came a row of trees. I pulled up and cleared them, then a small field and another row of trees. She still hadn't stalled, so I aimed her between two of the trees, which cut the wings off, and we collapsed onto a stone wall with a bump. The wall cut the nose of the Horsa clean off, just behind where we were sitting, but didn't damage the load or the passengers, although I think we were all a bit shaken.

Staff Sergeant Dodd and Sergeant M. Keeley were members of Musitano's and Perry's Flight. In a statement about the fate of the latter's glider Dodd recalled:

Having landed on the L.Z. and unloaded safely we proceeded to the first R.V. on the TROARN-RANVILLE road. We took up defensive positions in a German strong point on the East of the L.Z.

While we were here, and at approximately 0500hrs, S/Sgt. Musitano and Sgt. Perry entered the pillbox. They appeared very badly shaken, and they informed us that they had crashed on landing about 1000 yds. N.E. of RANVILLE, in a small field surrounded by an 8ft brick wall.

They were carrying a 6pdr. Ant-Tank Gun and Jeep, which they reported was still in the Glider, so I and Sgt. Keeley taking about 6 Paratroopers with us, set off to try and retrieve the Gun. On arriving at the scene we found the Glider in a very bad state. The mainplanes had been ripped off; the nose had been torn away and the rest of the fuselage had been embedded in the ground at an angle of 40 degrees.

We attempted for about three quarters of an hour to retrieve the Gun out of the wreckage, but found it impossible to do so by hand. The Paratroopers informed us that they could not hang on any longer and departed. I instructed S/Sgt. Musitano to stay with the Glider and that I would see if we could arrange to get some further help. I informed a Royal Engineer Officer of the position and he promised to do what he could.

Musitano and Perry eventually got their load out as Musitano explained:

We made our way to our appointed rendezvous in the company of a young gunner lieutenant, who said he would show us where he wanted the gun positioned. He came with us up a hilly lane between high banks, and as we neared the top, he made a remark which later I thought a bit odd. He said 'Keep your heads down, we may come under fire.' The lane was now on the same level as a large rectangular field on our right, into which we now turned and drove parallel to the lane we had just come up. We then made a left turn along the rear hedgerow, where perhaps half a company of troops were in position, another left turn at the end of this hedge and now opposite our entry point right down the far side of the field, where we again turned left and he, the gunner lieutenant, told us to position our gun in a ditch in a small copse. He then left us. It was then I remembered his 'keep your head down' bit. If we were likely to be fired on, then we were obviously being observed during that long trip around the field.

I suppose it was about six a.m. when we heard, and then saw, a German tank approaching. The gunner sergeant had earlier decided to go on a recce to our left. I forget why, but we never saw him again. The two gunners elevated the gun to bear on the tank, .only to discover it was so positioned, that with maximum elevation if it was fired, that the shell would have buried itself in the ground about fifty yards away. We saw movement to our right, beyond the edge of the field, and I lay on my belly with the Bren gun, back from the copse, and deliberately fired low at their legs, hoping to discourage rather than kill. From where the tank had been, some mortar shells began to fall on the copse. We discussed what to do and as I was now senior NCO, I gave the order to take the breech block from the useless gun, get back to the jeep and hare back down the field.

What happened next is vague. As we ran for the jeep we came under rifle fire from one of the flanks. One bullet seared by backside and hurt hellishly. Another grazed my spine and the pain in my arse went! One of the shots killed Paddy Perry, although I did not know about this until much later. I seem to remember the jeep starting up, but never discovered what happened to the gunners. I do not know how long the partial paralysis lasted, but as I lay there thinking I was going to die, although married, my first thoughts were sadness for my mother—I was her first. I remember burying by pretty little dagger in the ground beneath me—not a good thing to have if I was going to be captured. If a French farmer eventually dug it up it would not have been in good nick! I don't think they were made of stainless steel. It was getting hot, probably between eight or nine o'clock, when two very young German soldiers gingerly approached me. I could not know what they said between themselves, but whatever, the upshot was they carried me, all eleven stone, through the copse and into a cornfield. They went through my kit establishing what was army issue, took what was, including my watch, but after some deliberation decided that my lighter was not and gave it back to me. They did not find my escape kit sewn inside the bottom of my left trouser leg.

It was fortunate we were in a field of corn standing high, because about now, we came under fire from advancing British troops. I don't know how far we crawled and eventually walked— the paralysis had passed—but I was taken to a German Field Hospital where a doctor examined my wounds, probably treated them, and pinned a label on my camouflage jacket. No idea what was on the label, but it was probably just a diagnosis with treatment recommended. That I am writing this in 1979 is proof that I was in the hands of the German Army, observing the terms of the Geneva Convention to the letter.

Bill Musitano's great friend Sandy Dow, in Chalk 100, found that his landfall was further east than was desirable:

In the pre-take off briefing it had been suggested that the heavy anti-aircraft units at Le Havre should be given a wide berth, so it was somewhat surprising that this mini-airborne unit had, as its first identifiable sighting of the European coast, a fairly large urban setting which appeared to be Le Havre itself! There was radio communication silence from the tug plane, which appeared to bear west in the correct direction. Whether this lack of communication was official radio silence or 'traumatic', I don't know, but that concern became secondary to great difficulty maintaining formation as we entered much heavier cloud. Whatever happened next remained a mystery to me as we found ourselves in free flight.

In his Glider Raid Report, the tug pilot, Flying Officer Nickel, states that he released the glider in thick cloud as it had pulled 'the aircraft half way round and ... glider went up higher than aircraft and picked up aircraft's tail.' The tug could not identify the position at which they released the Horsa. Dow's immediate problem was finding somewhere to land the glider:

The quest was to find a substitute landing zone urgently, knowing from briefings that many of the fields had telegraph pole obstacles to thwart such a hope—and all in moonlight in foreign soil. We came down near Bouganville, landing quite heavily, but otherwise unscathed—albeit dazed, as the floor and frontage of the cockpit had smashed into some object on landing, and we found ourselves suspended by our safety straps—there being no floor or lower glazed part of the cockpit left. After all, Horsa gliders were well named 'matchbox' for, well-constructed as they were, laminated plywood was a major component and for the most part they were intended to be expendable in true action.

On French soil, well off the official drop-zone, we began to extricate ourselves. The tail part of the fuselage was damaged and to some extent this was to impede the extraction of the load. We were on agricultural land, with the odd midden and some larger farm buildings nearby. Unstrapped and somewhat staggery, we began collecting essential equipment with the intent of heading west for the correct destination.

Then came gunfire from all around and nearby and Dick Chadwick doubled up in pain, complaining of an abdominal gunshot wound. As I helped him against some building and was leaning over him tending his wound, we were quite suddenly surrounded by German troops, all pointing largish weapons at our temporarily undefended selves. Some of the neighbouring infantry seemed to shout 'Kamerad', but I was not given the time to make any such decision, and was marched off at gunpoint by several Germans, who would not allow me to stay with Dick, who appeared grievously wounded. Ignominy indeed, it all seems with hindsight, but all this happened in a matter of minutes to two dazed and just extricated men, one of whom was wounded. By, I presume, 0300 hours of D-Day I was to acquire the title of POW.

On the way to the first site of incarceration, I remember one scene where the three of us were lined up against a wall, hands above heads. The Germans, a few yards back, were all shouting vociferously. Beyond 'Essen' and 'Wasser' I spoke little German and have often wondered if they were arguing whether or not to shoot us. There was some debate amongst us, reference the possibility of making a run for it, but we decided that discretion was the better part of valour.

Sandy Dow's glider had hit an electricity transformer as it made its approach. The Germans had a watchpoint in a nearby church tower and saw everything. What is more, they were billeted in the farmhouse adjacent to where the glider landed. Seventeen-year-old Robert Marie and his sister looked after Chadwick, who was laid on the floor of the farmhouse by the Germans. The eighteen-year-old girl was holding his hand as he died. Robert is still indignant at the way the Germans treated the body:

Despite the pleas of my mother to bury the soldier according to our customs, those brutes decided to put him in the ground like a dog. They didn't want to 'waste' the sheet which we had wrapped around him as a shroud.

Staff Sergeant Downing, the first pilot of Chalk 118, must have been praying that his glider didn't land in the Channel. Ten minutes before take-off a member of the gun detachment carried on the glider, managed to inflate the emergency dinghy accidentally and burst it. As no replacement was available they took off without one, even though Downing's Mae West was also unserviceable! The flight across the Channel was uneventful until the coast was reached and a considerable amount of flak was experienced. Downing reported that only one light on the base of the 'T' was showing and that this went out as soon as he had cast off. As they made for the LZ the glider was engaged by more light flak, receiving strikes in the fuselage, wings and cockpit. A spare can of petrol, carried on the jeep, was holed and flooded the glider with petrol. The Horsa landed just fifty yards inside the LZ and took an hour and a half to unload.

Staff Sergeant Jolliffe and Sergeant Prentice, in Chalk 120, struck something at 100 feet as they made their approach to the LZ. The whole of the starboard side of the cockpit was smashed as was the pneumatic system and starboard stick. Touching down at 80 mph the glider, whose brakes were now useless, careered along the LZ and crashed into a hedge. Because of the damage, the crew had to blow the tail off to remove the gun and jeep.

In Chalk 112, Staff Sergeant Statham and Sergeant Boswell, had a rather rough landing on the LZ. Statham had to pull the nose up at the last minute, to avoid two other gliders on the ground, and his Horsa stalled at fifteen feet. The impact knocked off the nose wheel and port main wheel, although crew, passengers and load were all undamaged. The tail proved difficult to remove and finally had to be chopped through one longeron, the bolts being removed on the other three. Borrowing a set of unloading troughs from another glider, as their own were inaccessible, the crew tried to unload the jeep. Half way down the ramp, the starboard trough collapsed, forcing the crew to manhandle the vehicle the rest of the way. Because of damage to the ramp the gun had to be wrestled through the side loading door.

A number of 'D' Squadron's gliders landed away from the LZ. Major Lyne, the OC, landed near the River Dives and, despite a broken foot, marched to LZ 'N' to take over his command. There were by now, gliders being discovered all over the place. Henry Humberstone, a private in 224 Parachute Field Ambulance, had been dropped by parachute into the flooded area of the Dives valley:

Through the dark and wet night I struggled, picking up stragglers from different units. We were about six or seven strong and when daylight finally came we also reached dry ground and began to survey the surrounding countryside, to obtain some bearing toward our DZ. Then someone noticed the white stripes on an aircraft in the distance and as we got closer we could see that it was a glider.

A local Maquisard approached us and gave us warning of German troops billeted in the area. Up close the glider was broken, but not parted. Its front half was sloping downwards to a deep stream, and its back resting partly on the ground alongside the stream. It looked as though the pilot had been about to land the glider on the open field in view, but caught the tree and was slewed round into it.

Before we had the chance to survey the area more closely, we were approached by a lady who, we presumed, came from the house nearby. She invited us in, where we discovered Staff Sergeant Hunter, the first pilot of the Horsa, who was in bed with a broken leg. We made the pilot as comfortable as we could by splinting the broken leg and attending to his needs regarding cigarettes, rations etc., and thanking his French hosts for their kind assistance.

Returning to the crash area, we proceeded to collect the bodies of the occupants of the glider, scattered about the area, and laid them in a neat row, covered them and removed identity discs to be passed to the Padre of our unit later. The front of the glider had been smashed open and the body of the second pilot, Sergeant Stonebanks, was floating in the water. He too was laid to rest with the others.

On further examination of the glider we found it contained a jeep in the forward section and still attached, but leaning back towards the tail, a trailer. We made many attempts to separate them, but found it impossible to release the link.'

Six out of the seven people on 110 died when it hit the tree near the farmhouse at Briqueville. Some days later, Hunter was taken by the local priest in a horse-drawn cart in search of an Allied field dressing station. They were however, captured by a German patrol and the pilot was sent to a German military hospital in Paris where his displaced hip and badly broken leg were treated by a doctor. After a few days he was loaded with other wounded into some cattle trucks and left in a railway siding pending evacuation to Germany. He and a Scottish soldier by the name of O'Connell, were rescued by the Resistance, who attacked the train, and taken to a French hospital in Paris. Staff Sergeant Hunter returned to the United Kingdom in September but played no further part in the War, being awarded an eighty per cent War Disability Pension as a result of the injuries received in the crash.

Private Tony Leake of the 8th Parachute Battalion was part of a cover party for 3 Parachute Squadron R.E., who were to blow up the Dives bridges at Bures:

When they were nearly ready to blow up the bridges we crossed and went to see a Horsa glider which had crashed at 0345 hours in the river about a hundred yards south of the signal box, its nose on the western bank. Its load was a six-pounder anti-tank gun and jeep to tow it.

It carried a crew of three gunners of 4th Airlanding Anti-Tank Battery of the Royal Artillery in addition to the two glider pilots. One of the pilots had broken both his legs, each in two places, and two of the gunners were badly injured. The other pilot and one of the gunners were missing. As we arrived, the injured pilot was being lifted out of his cockpit and was in terrible pain. The poor man looked like a rag doll as his fractures were so bad. They put him on a stretcher and he and the two gunners were driven off to the 224 Parachute Field Ambulance dressing station at Le Mesnil. I believe the pilot survived, despite his dreadful injuries.

Then we went back to the Horsa and helped to try to pull the gun out of the wreckage, but this proved impossible, even after harnessing a horse and attaching chains. The jeep could not be removed either, as it was behind the gun.

This was almost certainly Chalk 102 of 'D' Squadron's Captain Walker and Sergeant Carpenter. The tug pilot must have mistaken the River Dives for the River Orne and released the Horsa in the wrong place, for they were five miles to the south-east of Ranville. Captain Walker and one of the gunners, who were the only ones uninjured in the landing, set off for the rendezvous, leaving the injured in the glider, as instructed in briefing. Somewhere along their route they were intercepted by the Germans and the Captain wounded and taken prisoner. The fate of the gunner is not known.

LZ 'N' was now secure and the anti-tank screen in place. It now remained for the pilots and the other airborne soldiers, dug in around the Ranville area, to see what the Germans intended to do about their presence.

Chapter Eleven

The morning and afternoon of 6 June was spent in a variety of tasks. 'Force John', under the command of Major John Royle, had been ordered to consolidate LZ 'N'. As soon as they had landed, the glider pilots assisted in the unloading of their aircraft, remaining with the airborne troops they carried until first light. The pilots, with the exception of those from 'D' Squadron, then moved to an RV in the wood, at grid 113735, and while some pilots prepared a defensive position, the remainder assisted the REs to clear additional landing strips on the LZ. This task completed, they occupied their positions and awaited the main lift of *Mallard*, which was scheduled for late evening and comprised 146 gliders for LZ 'N' and 108 for LZ 'W'. The 'D' Squadron crews remained under the command of the OC of 4th Airlanding Anti-Tank Battery, helping to man the six-pounders, until they were relieved by the original gunners.

For those crews who landed off target, or who had to move out to another RV, the night had been anything but dull. Andy Andrews' move towards the 3rd Parachute Brigade rendezvous, which was situated at a brickworks to the south of Le Mesnil, in the company of other members of his flight was one such journey:

We decided that while Taffy Lovett and I went ahead on either side of the road, the two jeeps were to follow behind, carrying the others at a safe distance. The orders to the drivers were to make for Ranville with the jeeps if we ran into any trouble, while we gave them covering fire. We came to the crossroads and, turning our back on Ranville, headed east. After about fifteen minutes we came to a small hamlet. Taffy stayed on the outskirts with the jeeps drawn into the hedge about a hundred yards back, while I crept cautiously along the street. It was more difficult to walk quietly now, and I was relieved when I came out on the road again at the other side. In a few minutes the rest of the party were through and we continued along the road, which now seemed to rise slightly.

About ten minutes later, as we approached another crossroads which could now be seen as it was beginning to get light again, a sudden burst of firing came from a light automatic weapon immediately to our front and a little to our left. We halted, and then decided as there was no further noise, to make for the trees. They turned out to be the entrance to the drive of a house which was our destination, the dawn rendezvous. The jeeps backed cautiously into the bushes at the side and we hastily dug a few holes as a small defensive position. It was quite light now, and round the bend of the drive came the middle-aged lady of the house. She showed no surprise at seeing us, and said that over the road there was an injured soldier to whom she was taking some wine.

The holes dug, we decided to investigate the shooting, and a small patrol consisting of the Major, Paddy and myself with one of the signallers cautiously approached the crossroads. On reaching them, we decided to turn left along what appeared to be the fence of the house which had been selected as the HQ. The right-hand bank was quite high, with a hedge bordering it and on the left a similar bank, terminating in a wire fence, which made it impossible to climb quickly. Through force of habit we walked on the left, at about arms-length intervals, and had proceeded about seventy-five yards down the road when a noise resembling the low note of a cow call attracted our attention on the other side of the road. We stopped, listened again, but there were no further noises. Then, after another two paces, I turned round to the Major and said 'I believe it's groaning,' He said, 'Maybe. Challenge.'

I still had my head turned in the direction from which we had come, when I said in a fairly normal tone 'Punch'. A voice replied 'Wer ist das' and followed it up, before we could have answered, even if we had wanted to, with a burst of automatic fire. The bullets went up the road behind us by about ten yards and by the time the last one had bedded itself in the bank, we were all lying full-length in a ditch with a very strong gravelly bottom, about 18 in wide and 18 in deep, and facing in the wrong direction. To make matters worse our rifles were useless and even if we could have seen where the fire came from, there didn't seem to be a target. I had a grenade in my pocket and seeing that the Major had one arm free, I passed it back to him. He removed the pin, waited for what seemed like an eternity, and then threw it. The explosion took place where we judged the firing had come from.

We waited for an answering burst but none came, and so very gingerly we turned round and began to retrace our steps towards the crossroads, one at a time, only this time crawling in the ditch. My hands and knees were sore for days afterwards, and when I stood up to run the last ten yards, I fell over again with cramp, but we all got safely round the corner and back to our HQ.

We felt that next time we should make a pincer movement, one from either side of the road, but from the height of the bank. We had chosen another two men, but before we could start on this little war of our own, the lady of the house came back and we decided to question her as to the whereabouts of the Germans. She informed us that next door there was an HQ with about seventy-five Germans. That explained the sentry we must have disturbed, and it rather changed our plans. The Major and one of the others went off to decide the best way to attack the house, while the rest of us decided to have a brew-up. Paddy started to prepare and I decided to go to the entrance of the drive and look down the road. I was observing from the cover of some bushes, when along the road towards us came a party headed by two glider pilots, with what looked like their passengers. They hadn't seen me yet, and when they were almost opposite, they sat down on the side of the bank with their backs towards me. I could have touched them, but I said 'Hello' instead. Their faces were a picture of surprise! Nevertheless, we now had some more reinforcements and they came back to our hide-out to rest.

The next to arrive on the scene were the RAMC. They were in a party of about forty strong and had a Polish prisoner with them. He was a youngster and nearly died of fright a moment or two later, when the pattern bombing of the beaches started. Even at the distance we were inland, the ground shook as though a miniature earthquake was in progress. The senior officers now took command and decided to send us, the glider pilots, back to Ranville with a report of the position. There we were to rejoin the glider pilot pool of reserves which had been formed.

We started out cautiously, walking parallel to the road. We passed a sentry, who only just recognised us in time, and later saw what we took to be our own paratroopers picking up supplies which had been dropped— only to find out later that they were probably Jerries after all, as we had no troops in the position. We made our way through the village, which was looking a bit sorry for itself, and passed a badly damaged glider which had hit a stone wall. We met a couple of newspaper reporters in the street and they directed us to the Divisional HQ which had been set up in the outhouses of a farm, the approaches of which were already under fire by snipers—we found that out after a near miss.

Having made our report to the General, we found a small corner behind some bushes and had a really wonderful cup of tea, made from provisions taken from our 48-hour ration pack. Then, much refreshed, we moved off to the glider pilot rendezvous, where there were twenty to thirty glider pilots. The main intention was that on arrival of the main lift at 2100 hours that evening, all pilots should be taken to England as quickly as possible to get ready for another trip. Meanwhile all we had to do was wait. We dug a hole, Paddy and I, and had some more to eat. There was spasmodic firing in the direction of Caen, and now and again patrols were sent out to contact the troops immediately to our front and flank, and so the day passed.

As the time for the main force grew near, the firing from the Germans grew louder, and the perimeter appeared to be hard pressed. I learned later that the gliders were late, and that they arrived at a very critical time. Eventually, above the noise of the firing, we heard the approach of many aircraft, the engines became a roar, and the firing seemed to cease. Even the Germans were struck dumb by what they saw. It was a magnificent sight, the air full of gliders sweeping in towards the German lines and then turning lazily and making a left hand circuit over our slit trenches. They seemed very low, and yet none of them appeared to be hit by the ground fire. After that perfect silence from the enemy, an absolute inferno of noise broke out. Our position, which up to that time had not come under fire, was plastered with mortars, as Jerry tried to get the range of the landing zone. This forced us to keep our heads down, but we could still hear the whistle of the gliders as they continued to land.

Later, after the firing had died down, I crawled cautiously to the high ground overlooking the landing zones. The area was covered with gliders, a beautiful 'Balbo', which earned for it the name of the 'Milk Run'. Out of curiosity I glanced over to my own landing position a little to the right of the main body. I was surprised to see that what I had thought to be my brake binding, had in fact been the wing of the glider knocking over an anti-invasion pole. My luck must have been terrific for the glider had only touched this one pole, and had steered a course between the others without my having known that they were there.

We decided to keep watch alternatively during the night, not because we were in any immediate danger, in our position, of being taken by surprise, but because we felt that we should keep up appearances for other wandering units who, not appreciating our exertions of the night before, might take a poor view if they found us asleep. I took a benzedrene, which is supposed to keep you awake—at least I thought so, but I was overcome with sleep in about five minutes and had just enough time to kick Paddy awake. The next thing I knew he was kicking me, and my first vision was of planes flying over and dropping parachutes. We had been warned that Jerry might try an immediate counter-attack with his own parachutists, and that managed to get through to me. For the rest of the night I kept awake, and found with relief just before dawn, that they were our own Dakotas dropping supplies. The next morning, quite early, we had orders to prepare to march to the beach-head.

Lieutenant Chris Dodwell was in another slit trench in the defensive perimeter:

A little to our right was a six-pounder anti-tank gun, brought in by one of the gliders during the night. Several of its crew had been killed and it was being operated by a mixed group of glider pilots and its own gunners. A noisy battle was going on as German tanks tried to break through towards the bridges over the River Orne and the Caen Canal. This gun destroyed four out of the five German tanks making this attack. Later on, a German 88 mm gun started firing at targets on the landing zone behind us. Unlike most other guns, which fired their shells up in the air to some degree, the 88 fired a very high velocity shell which travelled more or less parallel to the ground until it reached its target. If it was firing at close range the shells never got very high and the rounds from this gun were going through the top of the hedge above us and covering us with broken twigs and branches.

Our own position then enjoyed a bit of a lull until the main lift arrived. The German fire became intense, but the gliders came steadily in, their wings with the black and white invasion markings catching the evening sun. Somewhere near us, a German machine-gun was firing non-stop. Then occurred a strange incident. A Horsa flew over us with a tow-rope trailing over its wing. This rope should have been dropped by the tug aircraft well clear of the landing zone, but this one must have been dropped prematurely by a tug and landed on the glider. As the Horsa turned directly over us, the rope slipped off and came down on the spot where the German machine-gun was firing from. Now a tow-rope consisted of pretty heavy hempen rope and three heavy metal plugs, by means of which it was attached to the tug and glider. When dropped, they hit the ground with considerable force. Whether it hit the German position or not, I couldn't see, but the gun stopped and did not fire again.

The morning of the 6th was a busy time for the pilots of 'D' Squadron who had brought in the anti-tank guns, as illustrated in the reports they filled in on return to the UK, describing the German attacks which probed the perimeter defences. Staff Sergeant Downing's report is short and to the point:

We dug into position and were not bothered by enemy activity until about 1030 hours, when enemy mechanised (two tanks and two self-propelled guns) and infantry appeared. Our six-pounder scored a hit on one of the tanks with the first round, from about 600 yards, and the second round blew it up. The infantry were repulsed, mainly by the 13th Para. Bn., but I'm certain I nailed one Jerry and possibly two.

For the remainder of D-Day we were fired on spasmodically by snipers, light and heavy machine-gun fire, mortars and light artillery. Our jeep suffered a direct hit from mortars, and although we saved the jeep by throwing off the burning kit, a great deal of equipment and ammunition (including my ammunition) was destroyed.

The gun of Staff Sergeant Rickwood and Sergeant Gray accounted for an armoured car which was towing a gun. The crew of Chalk 115, Staff Sergeant White and Sergeant Eason, became involved in a vicious fire fight around 0830 hours:

Co-pilot on look-out observed enemy tank movement on our left flank. Our gun well concealed, but not very well sited. We came under small arms fire and Sergeant Eason opened up on the Bren gun. By this time first S.P tanks (sic) in range of gun, but gun layer did not consider that he could hit the tank. In the meantime, I had loaded a round and had a look through the sights myself. By this time the tank was almost dead in front at 200 yards range and needed stopping, so I decided to have a go myself Sergeant Eason kept the Nazis' heads down by Bren fire and layed the gun ready to fire. The first round missed and so I immediately reloaded and this time applied 200 range on the sights. The tank had stopped and I was expecting them to open up on us at any minute, so I quickly sighted the gun and fired. This time it was a hit and the tank went up in flames. During this short time another tank had been hit by the gun on the left flank and also, one that was almost unobserved from our position, was put out of action by a gun on our right flank. From our position, three tanks were seen to be burning, and ammo was exploding in each at varied intervals. The infantry, who were escorting the tanks, were then engaged for the remainder of the day by small arms fire.

Captain B. Murdoch, whose first flight had been aborted over Winchester, moved his anti-tank gun to a position in a hedgerow a mile to the south of Ranville at 0330 hours on the 7th, and together with members of 12th Parachute Battalion, waited for the German reaction. At noon the Germans attacked:

Jerry attacked our left flank, keeping us to our slit trenches with M.G. and mortar fire. I was observing for the gun and saw a tank which was firing H.E. and M.G. I explained the position of it, but the gun detachment would not open fire. At last I persuaded them and I loaded the gun. The layer scored a hit and put the tank Mk IV out of action. It was burning furiously and I did not see anyone get out of it. Another tank spotted us and opened fire with M.G., forcing us to take to the slit trenches. The tank fired H.E., which killed the layer, gun detachment commander and wounded the driver. I ordered the paratroopers to move up the hedge to a new position. I sent for stretcher-bearers, meanwhile applying first aid to the gun detachment commander, who was dying, and then to the jeep driver. I asked for volunteers to keep the gun in action and a Para sergeant said that he would come over shortly. I then saw another tank and ran to the gun. The target was moving, so I aimed on its nose, but missed. It turned for home and was at once hit by another gun. As the tank commander got out, we opened fire on him and then the tank blew up. I found the gun breech wide out and it would not return on its slide. The recuperator had been locked and the gun was u/s. We took the jeep with the breech block, which I had removed from the gun, and all remaining ammunition and salvageable kit belonging to dead and wounded gunners, to Divisional HQ and reported to Commander Royal Artillery, pointing out the position of the gun.

Throughout the 7th, parties of glider pilots had been sent to the beach to embark for the UK. Chris Dodwell led the point patrol of one of these groups:

We formed up for our march towards the beaches. The usual formation was for a small patrol of two or three to lead the way, followed by a section, while the main body followed on behind. I found myself, with Staff Sergeant Andrews and Sergeant Senier, nominated for the position of leading patrol.

As we led the way along the raised road toward the bridges over the River Orne and the Caen Canal, we could see dead cattle and horses lying in the fields, their legs stuck up stiffly in the air. By the bridges themselves, were the gliders which had made the surprise attack by night, during which the bridges had been seized. On the far side of the bridges we entered the area which the main seaborne forces had passed through the day before. Devastation was everywhere, with ruined buildings and wires trailing in the streets. Approaching the village of Colleville, we halted while a tank blasted at a tall church steeple, from which a German sniper had been firing.

As we neared the beaches we met the German minefields, their boundaries marked with skull and cross bones signs and the warning 'Achtung Minen '. Wide paths, marked with white tape, had been cleared through them by the British 'Flail' tanks to allow the seaborne forces to push inland. In between the mine-fields were the concrete fortifications of the 'Atlantic Wall', now shattered by the bombing and shelling, which we had heard the previous day from ten miles inland.

On the beach were piles covered by tarpaulins, from which one could see now and then, a pair of black boots protruding, very still. In a sheltered corner stood a group of dishevelled German prisoners. Below the high water line stood the steel obstructions in the form of three-legged 'X's, to hinder landing craft. The sky was low and grey as we waited on the beach for a landing ship to nose in and take us off. A German fighter aircraft dived out of the cloud and flew along the beach, pursued by a couple of Spitfires. Eventually, a landing ship came and we waded out through the shallow water to climb aboard. At the water's edge there were still bodies brought in by the waves.

We had had little rest or sleep in the last two and a half days and we fell exhausted into the bunks. We were not yet allowed to relax, as a Focke-Wulf 190 fighter-bomber made a series of attacks on our ship. Between the noise of the ship's engines alternately going ahead and astern as it dodged the bombs and the racket of its anti-aircraft guns, rest was impossible. At last the F. W. was driven off and silence fell. I have little recollection of the rest of the voyage.

The next morning was still grey and overcast as we came into Newhaven. Stiff and dirty, we climbed into lorries which would take us to our Regimental Depot on Salisbury Plain for debriefing, and later back to Down Ampney to regroup and reorganise in readiness for the next operation.

Aubrey Pickwoad moved down to the beaches about the same time:

With my party of eight glider pilots we had to escort a party of about one hundred and fifty Jerries to Divisional HQ. When we had them all lined up I told one of the lads, whom I knew spoke a bit of German, to inform the prisoners that if any of them made the slightest move to escape that they would be shot. Most of them burst out laughing! When our German-speaking lad asked them what was up, he was told that there would be no attempt to escape, as all they wanted was to get to England as soon as possible! On our way to Div. HQ, we passed a jeep with three Para lads in it. It had received a direct hit and the lads had been thrown some yards from the jeep, killed instantly by the blast. One of them was kneeling face down, and out of his right-hand back jacket pocket protruded the top of a Penguin paperback book, the title of which was' Why Britain is at War'. It would have made 'The' poignant picture of the War, had I had a camera.

After handing over the prisoners we set off to the west. We passed General Browning on the way dressed, as usual, as if he were on Horse Guards Parade. As we crossed the bridge over the Caen Canal there was still a bit of firing going on, but as it didn't appear to be aimed at us we carried on. On the way a friendly farmer gave us some cider, or that's what he said it was. We had not had much to drink for the last two days, so down it went and by the time we got to the beach we were quite happy!

Fred Baacke, in the company of Roy Howard, had been given permission to make his way to the beach shortly after the main force landed at 2100 hours:

We walked along the road to Ouistreham and came to a wood in which there seemed to be thousands of Glider Pilots. We walked on—with visions of brown blanco for the trees, green blanco for the grass and see that you get the barbed wire polished à la Tilshead! We arrived outside the town at dusk, with a big air raid in progress and the Allied Fleet putting on the most impressive firework display I've ever seen. We slept in a field until dawn and then pressed on for the beach, where we introduced ourselves to the Beachmaster. Ships stretched from the shore to the horizon, a cheering sight, especially when the battle wagons far out at sea were pumping shells into either Le Havre or Cherbourg.

Ray and I stretched out for a sleep on the beach, when a clot with a Bofors promptly knocked the tail off a marauding Ju 88. This made a three-point landing (nose and two wing tips!) in the midst of the beach and about sixty yards from us. The lot immediately went up in flames, to the accompaniment of exploding small arms ammunition. With my teeth and finger nails, I dug a slit trench, fully six inches square and deep, and emulated the ostrich. When the blaze died down, Colonel Murray, with his aides, and followed by the full force of the Glider Pilot Regiment, strolled by. One of the aides, seeing me, called me to come to him. I limped over, having hurt my leg, and was promptly ordered to 'double'. I made a quick mental note, doubting his ancestral origin, and I think, he read my mind.

Thereafter, we loaded on to an Infantry Landing Craft after wading through the sea and ruining my supply of cigarettes. I said 'How do' and had a short chat to an individual whose face looked familiar to me. Roy looked aghast and amazed. He informed me later that the individual was the renowned 'Tojo', the RSM. I apologised to him for my effrontery and familiarity as I did not recognise him in his war paint, so different from his usual immaculate turnout.'

While most of the glider pilots on the landing ships were enjoying their first experience of a bed for three days, others from the squadrons were not so fortunate.

Chapter Twelve

While the other pilots of his squadron were helping to man the anti-tank guns, Bill Musitano was beginning his period of captivity:

I was loaded into an ambulance the next morning with three German soldiers, one of whom had horrific groin wounds. We were going south and after a few miles we were, on the ground, mixed with a military convoy going north. The convoy was strafed by American aircraft firing .50 calibre bullets. Our ambulance, with two of its tyres deflated and the driver and his mate flat in a ditch, was stationary opposite what turned out to be a school. No-one in the ambulance had been hit. My jacket sported wings—not well known for being different from the RAF or US wings. I was the most mobile of the ambulance's occupants, but probably my wings prompted me to help the three Germans out of the ambulance and into the school.

We were in the school for two or three hours—the time it took the ambulance crew to repair the damage to the tyres. Later that day we got to a village called Aunay-sur-Odon and were put to bed in a very small hospital, about the size of an English cottage hospital—the beds touched. I saw the name of the village again in an RAF Mess many months later. It was on an aerial photograph showing the little village had been the centre of a Panzer Division, and all one could see was covered in bomb craters. This bombing by Lancasters had taken place on the night of 8th June 1944. In Aunay we were taken to a village hall mentioned above as a small hospital and we were tended by local girls and women on whom I practised my French.

We were awakened early next morning and I had enough French to understand that walking wounded were being moved on. About a dozen of us, of various nationalities, clambered aboard an open lorry in which a lot of hay had been scattered to make our next journey not too uncomfortable. So we left Aunay on the morning of 8th June and travelled, entirely through lanes, in a south-westerly direction. Our first stop was at a chateau, which was being used as a casualty clearing station, and it was here that the German wounded were separated from the Allied. At this time I do not remember being hungry or thirsty, but at some time since leaving England food and drink must have been supplied, but what or where is a complete blank.

There were German soldiers at the chateau, but I was not subject to any interrogation—my uniform told them I was a pilot in the GPR. I slept soundly for some time in an outhouse. My third night in France was spent in a girls' school in Rennes, which had been turned into a hospital. We were a mixed bag of British, Canadian and American, but mostly British. This included my own flight commander, Captain Walker. All had wounds of varying degrees of severity and a few died, but not many considering that most had only received first aid before being examined by the surgeons at Rennes, 48 to 72 hours after the wounds had been inflicted. There were not many of them, but all the nurses were French and the elderly French surgeon who operated on me apparently knew his job. When my turn came I was taken to a room adjoining the theatre and told by one of the nuns present to strip entirely and a couple of them washed my back and bottom with surgical spirit. I then had to walk to the operating table and clamber on. I was given an anaesthetic, but apparently all the surgeon did was to tidy up the wound in my back, cover it with sulphanilamide and stick a plaster on. For several days afterwards, the only pain, or more accurately discomfort, was the pulling of my skin by the plasters. The dressing was never changed. Later an RAMC doctor in England, remarked on it, complimenting the French surgeon on his work.

The next five or six weeks are remembered mainly for being a time of continuous hunger—watery soup and black bread, dated on the base, was all we got. I had long since opened my escape kit and eaten the chocolate. But it also contained French money, so I was able to buy cigarettes brought in by one of the nurses, and also one very special occasion, a cake as I had discovered that when you are hungry the body craves sugar.

I had lost all my kit, so was now growing a beard. Apart from Captain Walker I remember only one man in the hospital. He was a Rhodesian Spitfire pilot who had been shot down and badly burned. He told me that Goering's personal surgeon had operated on his face before being sent to Rennes. My unusual surname and the fact that I lived in Cornwall must have stuck, as he visited me in my Falmouth pub ten years later—the scars still showed.

The Geneva Convention was, fortunately for me, being well observed in this area of conflict. After about six weeks I was pronounced, by one of the German doctors, fit to be discharged to the POW camp. But first I had to go before a panel for the discharge to be confirmed. This consisted of a German Captain, a German Lieutenant, but because he was the senior medical officer, one Major Oxley RAMC, himself a POW, sitting in the centre of the tribunal. He spoke first and to the point 'Ah yes, Musitano. You are a skilled carpenter are you not?' My knowledge of carpentry in 1944 consisted almost entirely in knowing he was talking about wood! My narrative up to this point may suggest I was a trifle shell-shocked, but I had the sense to answer 'Yes Sir'. The Major continued—'The Camp Commandant tells me he needs a craftsman to take charge of the Algerian carpenters. Can you do the job?' Again 'Yes Sir.'

I do not know if Major Oxley had received any directives to delay the discharge of any POWs who were pilots, or others whose training took months rather than weeks, but that encounter was the first time I had met him. Later, for a reason I cannot remember, I borrowed five Pounds from him which I have never repaid. I was surprised that the Germans on the tribunal had not asked me if I spoke French, because the four or five Algerians I was put in charge of next morning spoke nothing else. However, my lack of expertise in carpentry or French was not insurmountable as I found a fellow POW with some knowledge of both. Our first job, building some shelves in the Camp Commandant's office, was completed—I think, to his satisfaction.

I was allowed to use the staff canteen, which had only three commodities—tinned tuna fish, granulated sugar and light French beer on draught. My first filling meal for over six weeks was perhaps a trifle too filling. I doubt if there are many who would tackle as a repast, two tins of tuna and half a kilo of sugar washed down with two litres of beer. I did, and was only slightly uncomfortable for a few hours. It recalls the time in Wethersfield when I had a ten Shilling bet with a young Jock Dow that he could not finish off the four ounces of butter, four ounces of cheese and a slice of cake in fifteen minutes flat, straight after we had finished our meal. I do not remember who paid! At the hospital it was a little odd to see tomato trays, obviously from the Channel Islands, marked 'British Produce' and packets of Swan Vestas. I suppose I carried out whatever jobs given me satisfactorily, because I was still there when the Americans arrived.

There was a large Red Cross on the school's roof and I do not think there were many German troops in the area, because the arrival of the Americans was preceded only by some light mortar fire. There was though, a Gestapo unit in a building next to the school and I was one of the few Allied troops who went into the place and took away a grey trilby hat, with a London maker's name inside, because it happened to be my size. Probably we were damn silly to have gone in, as the place might well have been booby-trapped. However, the Gestapo had left in a hurry, well before the Germans in the hospital. One of them was found in a cupboard when we were liberated—he had had enough of the war. The first truckload of supplies the U.S. Army delivered contained fifty percent plasma and fifty per cent cigarettes.

The next morning I decided to walk down into Rennes—we were on the outskirts. At first no-one took any notice of me, although I remember passing the time of day with a male and a female Gendarme, but I had not been walking very long when a citizen of Rennes accosted me and invited me into his house for breakfast. He lived alone and I now had my second, and vastly superior, memorable meal. It started off soberly enough: a large cup, almost a bowl, of excellent coffee and a large chunk of white French bread. He then produced a full plate a/very delicious ham and of all things, a bottle of rum. We each had a glass of this, but more was to come, for the next arrival was a bowl containing about a pound of strawberries and a bottle of Champagne. I think we finished the bottle between us and I am sure I thanked him profusely before continuing my exploration.

My next contact was an American G.I. He had no weapons and was possibly a deserter. He asked me where he could find a woman, explaining that he didn't know the local lingo. My French is far from good but I thought I had enough, no doubt fortified by the liquid content of my breakfast, to try to help him. I approached an elderly Frenchman: 'Bonjour, Monsieur. Mon ami l'Americain desire une fille de joi.' I was sure he was not getting the message and I was trying to enlarge on the subject, when from a first floor window just above us, a woman's voice said 'I'm English.' We looked up. 'The Boche closed all the brothels '. She advised us to try the nearby cafe and when we got there we ordered drinks. Public bars in Brittany in '44 were probably very badly stocked and what I drank was very reminiscent of some concoction I had been given in childhood as medicine. I don't remember if there were any women in the bar, but the G.I. seemed to have enough money on him to buy whatever he wanted, if only by signs. I left the bar and returned to the hospital.

Those not needing ambulances were transported by truck. The next day I was taken north to Avranches and then north-east to St. Lo. It was reassuring to see G.I. 'Snowballs' doing point duty at every intersection and surprising to pass a couple of American locomotives. I wondered at the time if they had been specially built to fit the French gauge. There was tremendous battle damage from Avranches north—whole towns and villages had been destroyed. I never learnt how many French civilians had been killed or wounded during the Liberation, but it surely must have been thousands.

At St. Lo we were given the run of a P.X. A lot of the stuff was second hand and I took a gabardine waist-length jacket with a zip front, as my battledress top had been cut up the back when I was first examined at the German field hospital on D-Day. I also took some razor blades, but did not shave off my beard until much later. We then queued up for food and as the weather was fine, ate it in the open. There was no rationing, so I took seven lamb chops, a pile of vegetables, a large helping of pineapple and cream and a mug of coffee. St. Lo was a clearing place for the US Army, so I was passed on to a British equivalent further west. My first meal there was a contrast—a tin of bully beef, some bread and a mug of tea. The tea however, even though it was a typical army brew, strong sweet and laced with tinned milk, went down better than American coffee.

I was in the transit camp somewhere near Bayeaux for a couple of days where I was debriefed. This was a perfunctory affair and only lasted a few minutes. I remember being disapproving of some of our lads who, perhaps because they had not been treated as well as I had by the Germans, had taken watches from the German POW's in the nearby stockade. Eventually, I was embarked in a small ship from a Mulberry harbour in the Baie de la Seine and went right across in a channel marked by buoys. We hoped the minesweepers had done a good job! We were each issued with a one man, fourteen day K-Ration pack. I had a very hot tin of self-heating soup and also ate most of a tin of what was very like Christmas pudding, pocketing the cigarettes, which were American. We disembarked and went up to London by train.

A large building in Marylebone was my next residence. Sober, I had my first bath in just over nine weeks. I had been told that V2s were landing in London, so when I went to bed that night, I selected a room on what I thought was the north side. The next day I was kitted out with a new battledress and a ghastly khaki bonnet and saw an M.O. He, as mentioned earlier, approved the treatment I had received and recommended fourteen days leave as the best step to full recovery. I was given travel documents and conveyed next morning to Paddington station. I had to telephone my wife in Cornwall, who told me that I had been posted missing, probably a POW. I was able to tell her on which train I should be arriving in Lostwithiel. The details of my journey are vague and for some stupid reason, I must have been dozing, for when the train pulled into Lostwithiel station I stayed in my seat, saw my wife and her mother on the platform and was unable to move myself in time before the train pulled out. The next stop was Par, four miles on, where my parents lived. I did get out there and my wife came down on the next train.

After my leave I was posted to a rehabilitation centre in Matlock Bath. I was there about ten days, saw a couple of M.O.s and underwent a few intelligence tests. I spent most of my time and two nights in Derby. I seemed to have plenty of money. A day in Derby usually consisted of a session in a pub in the morning, a cinema in the afternoon, and back to the pub or a hotel in the evening. I only remember two social contacts. I was asked to join a party one evening in someone's house and stayed the night, but not with my hostess. Another evening in an hotel I met Ivy Benson, who told me that she learnt a new language every year, which ability she put down to her musical ear. I left Matlock with a clean bill of health and rejoined my Squadron.

There was an embarrassing moment when, shortly after arriving, I was summoned to the CO's office. The Adjutant was there too. 'Glad to see you back, Musitano' said the CO in welcome. 'You had a rough time I believe.' I certainly had not! The only other things I remember being mentioned was his approval of my beard and being told that I could keep it. This was strictly against Kings Regulations, as only a Sergeant of Pioneers in an infantry regiment can wear a full set. There was also the awful moment when he said 'Sorry your second pilot was killed ... er ... what was his name?' I racked my brain and nothing came. Had Matlock been sure they were right to send me away? I said 'Sergeant ... . we called him Paddy.' (dammit—he had been my SP for three months). The CO tried to help. He was telling the Adjutant to look in a certain file when my brain unblocked. 'Perry, Sir—yes Sergeant Perry. He was from Eire.' Apart from that and the time I went to a railway booking office and asked for a ticket to somewhere I couldn't remember, and then not feeling up to attending my son's christening, for no explainable reason, my eight-hour war had been a piece of cake!

Bill Musitano wrote this account shortly before his death and thirty-five years after the events took place. People often remember things that made a great impact at the time in great detail. The names of places and people have blurred with the years, but the menus have remained crystal-clear. It must have been traumatic for a fit young man to have been so hungry for so long. He wasn't the only Glider Pilot at Matlock Bath. Three others from 'D' Squadron also travelled there—the long way.

Chapter Thirteen

Many of the crews from those gliders which had landed away from the LZs were captured by the Germans. Staff Sergeant Bryan Helme's Horsa had landed near Dozule, perhaps ten miles from the LZ. As the crew tried to remove the tail they were mortared and had to abandon the glider. The pilots and the five passengers split into two parties and started to make their way south-west towards Ranville. Bryan and two of the passengers were surprised and surrounded as they sheltered under a bridge and were forced to surrender. The former pilot still remembers the feeling of guilt he felt at the time at his capture.

Sandy Dow was taken by lorry to *Frontstalag* 153 at Verneuil, near Lisieux. It was at this purpose-built POW camp that he met up with two other glider pilots from 'D' Squadron, Bill Shannon and Bryan Helme. Sandy Dow described the camp:

It was a hutted encampment, rigorously surrounded by the hallmarks of imprisonment in the shape of barbed wire, high fencing and the traditional elevated guard posts. We were crowded, about eighty at a time, into huts where surprisingly, a metal army-type bedstead was allocated to each person. This was far superior to the initial place of confinement, where we spent the first two or three days in a kind of barn, crowded with nearly three hundred men. The only bedding was just crude palliasses and the latrine was at one end of the barn. The latter consisted of three largish dustbins, over which was placed a plank, and thus enthroned, the three lucky ones who had reached the head of the queue, had to perform their intimate exercise in the full glare of their other two hundred and ninety-seven comrades.

The huts were a distinct improvement, with a daily ration of vittals even. Twelve loaves of rye bread and hunks of sausage or a soupy potage would be the daily ration for the whole hut. This was augmented by a weakish brew of ersatz coffee—dandelion, I think, the taste of which I have never forgotten. Strangely enough, it was not entirely unpleasant. A routine was established for the collection of comestibles—volunteers a-plenty, while for the most distasteful tasks, such as emptying the latrines, a detail was the order of the day. The former duty was popular for another reason, as it permitted a certain mobility and change of scene. The aroma of the freshly baked loaves was tantalising, first thing in the morning and the camp kitchen staff, who were French girls, endeavoured from time to time, to slip in an extra loaf In these circumstances, a baker's dozen was bounty indeed! In this Frontstalag there were only about four or five glider pilots, who, by virtue of their senior rank, participated in the share-out of twelve to thirteen loaves between eighty men. Greedy eyes watched every morsel, and occasionally, when a stale loaf had been thrown in officially, any greenish, mouldy sections were set aside with the greatest of precision, while the remaining crumbs were virtually counted out amongst the luckiest participants of that day.

Rotas were established for cleaning duties and, even though this was a Frontstalag, opportunities were forever searched for the possibility of escape. Such were few at this time, for after all we were among the first Allied prisoners taken after the D-Day landings, most of us Airborne troops—prize indeed for the German High Command. This placement lasted approximately three weeks, but even in that short time, the effect of being a prisoner of war in enemy hands, the slight stigma of shame which attached to that misfortune, the actual incarceration, discomfort, lightness of rations, loss of liberty, overcrowding, reduced privacy and difficulty in personal hygiene, all compounded to bring out, sometimes the best, sometimes the worst in the varied personalities, with all the pre-existing traits tending to magnify.

There were incidents, even in this brief time. The brighter spirits organised exercises and prisoners who were 'expert' at anything gave lectures. Bill Shannon gave talks about his pre-war training as a cavalryman. One morning the bread collection detail returned murmuring disconsolately about only twelve loaves that day. Yet, long after lights out in the hutted darkness, a soldier heard the sounds of munching from under the blanket of his nearby comrade. The noise was investigated by pulling his neighbour's blanket down, to reveal fragments of a thirteenth loaf being voraciously chewed by that patently guilty sneak thief I cannot recall the punishment meted out, but he was certainly sent to Coventry and 'short of his ration' for a few days.

A classical interrogation took place in Chartres. This was individual and my predecessor came out of the room, which was a nearby school classroom, carrying a shovel over his shoulder.

From the playground later came the sound of shots, then shovelling. I was directed in and stood before a table, at which sat a suave, immaculately uniformed, Iron-Crossed German officer, who spoke

'Oxford-accent English'. He motioned me to sit down and, in a friendly fashion, offered me a Players cigarette which, although I did not smoke, I accepted. Cigarettes had great bartering value in any army unit, especially in a POW camp. Initially, he was pleasant and agreeable. His manner became more abrasive as he received nothing from me in answer, apart from the authorised name, rank and number. He showed me a list of southern English airfields with Tarrant Rushton underlined, asking me to confirm what he said that my friends had already told him, that this had been my point of embarkation. I repeated my name, rank and number, which appeared to irritate him and he removed a pistol from his belt and put it on the table, motioning a couple of heavies to come up behind me. Blessedly, outside the window I could see Chartres Cathedral framed in the setting sun the beauty of the scene balancing the threatening atmosphere inside the room. Presumably, when it became obvious to him that I wasn't spilling any beans, the interview suddenly terminated. There was no further threat and no actual violence and I wonder, with hindsight, if meekness on the behalf of the interrogee might have been the wedge which permitted them to extract further information. I was returned swiftly to the new accommodation at the school and informed that we would be embarking by truck to Paris and then by train to Germany, to a proper POW camp.

On the morning of 29 June, the three glider pilots were amongst the six hundred POWs loaded into ancient Renault buses and driven off in convoy towards Paris. Bill Shannon remembers the Allied reaction to the convoy:

In spite of the large red crosses painted on the roofs of the buses, we were strafed by a flight of Typhoons and casualties were sustained amongst the prisoners. The guards were safe in slit trenches at the side of the road, but we remained locked in the buses during the attack. The old buses, which had gazogen generators, frequently broke down and the POW's were required to dismount and push-start them. During the confusion, one of a group of French Paras managed to lift a screwdriver and a pair of pliers from a tool box.

The French Para wasn't the only soldier to benefit from the journey. Bryan Helme managed to purloin a short metal bar, which he had found under one of the seats on the bus. The POW's were to experience a welcome in Paris which they had not expected, as Bill Shannon recalls:

Arriving at the Gare du Nord, the convoy halted and we had to run the gauntlet through a hostile crowd of French civilians, who punched, kicked and spat at us. After forming up in the station yard we were marched, by a circuitous route round the city to the Gare de l'Est, which is only next door. We had to wait a long time in the sun and most of us were bursting for a pee. The many pleas to the guards to accommodate our needs were ignored and to add insult to injury, from the upstairs windows of an adjacent building, a large number of German women soldiers were hurling scathing comments in our direction. This was the final straw! It was almost as if the move had been choreographed. The massed ranks of prisoners smartly turned in the direction of these women, released their flies, and proceeded to relieve themselves, forcing the shrieking harpies to retire from the windows in disarray. The guards, however, were not amused and ran up and down shouting a lot!

Eventually, we were crammed into the usual cattle trucks. Before the doors were locked we were given hot soup, which was poured into our cupped hands and a piece of bread, which was to be our rations for the four days of our journey. Inside the trucks it was extremely hot and they held more than the nominal forty men. Some were sick or wounded and they lay on the floor, the rest taking turns sitting or lying. Sandy Dow, Bryan Helme and I, together with the French Paras, formed a little group in one corner. Soon, we had a shift system in operation, digging away at the two planks which held the ventilator closed. Unfortunately, the train stopped for the night and as the guards were patrolling both sides of the track, work had to stop. Another problem arose. A private in the Green Howards, learning that there was an escape plan, threatened to call the guards. He was afraid that those left behind would be shot in reprisal. Capitaine Jean Valois, the leader of the French, called the man a traitor and said he would make sure that the man was shot for treason on return to the UK. Early next morning the POW's were allowed out, a few trucks at a time, to attend to the wants of nature. The traitor had eventually carried out his threat, for before we remounted, we were subjected to a rigorous search and the tools were found on the French. Sadly, all the French Paras were taken away and locked in the next wagon, which had steel shutters. However, they had given us much useful information.

A ladle of coffee was issued and the train set off again. Once on the way, we carried on with the interrupted work on the planks using the metal bar which Bryan Helme had managed to retain. We had to work more cautiously now, so as not to arouse the suspicion of the prisoners nearby. By late evening we had removed all the wood surrounding the bent-over nails which held the inner and outer planks together. Now it was necessary to wait for dark before completing the job. Between us, we had a silk map of Northern France, a compass and 1400 French Francs. All the other items of our escape kits had been discovered piece by piece after many searches. While it was light we had noticed the station name board 'Reims', but with the light fading we were unable to read any of the subsequent station names.

We had drawn straws to decide who should go first and I drew the short one! As soon as it was really dark, the outer plank was pushed clear. The inner plank was used to beat the barbed wire flat and the barbs were covered with a piece of blanket which I had found in the Frontstalag. Sandy and Bryan took my legs and slowly pushed me through the narrow opening. I silently prayed that the train was not approaching a tunnel or a bridge, or that a guard would not look out of a carriage window. Finding a grab-handle, I was able to haul myself round onto the buffers and signal to the others to follow. The two pilots came out in quick succession, aided by some U.S. Engineers, who stayed behind.

For some time we rode the buffers, looking for a suitable embankment which we could roll down. The moon had risen and the countryside was bathed in silvery light. The train slowed down as it approached a station, rumbling through at walking speed. We were horrified to see our shadows cast on the platform, as we passed a sentry only feet away. Luckily, he must have been sunk into the stupor that affects many sentries in a safe area. A few miles from the station I saw a suitable embankment and jumped, thinking that the others would follow immediately. Unfortunately, I landed on the signal wires that ran down the side of the track and was catapulted back towards the train, landing on the ballast with my head a foot from the wheel.

As the train disappeared into the distance and I realised that I was still alive, I set off to find my companions. Ahead, I saw a dark figure outlined against the sky, so I whistled the agreed recognition signal. The reply was a surprise. There was a flash and a crack as a bullet whistled past me. Startled, I took off across the track, cleared a hedge and ran for several-hundred yards before hiding in a clump of trees. After about half an hour, the moon went behind a cloud and it all seemed quiet, so I set off once more to find my friends, for they had the map and compass. Approaching cautiously and using all my fieldcraft, I crept down to the railway again. Alas, in the dark, I didn't see the other set of signal wires and stumbled into them, setting them twanging in the distance. Once again I was fired at. I decided that there was no future in this, so abandoned the meet and, using the stars, set off in a southerly direction. I had not gone far, when I came across a road. This made for easier walking, but I soon heard the tramp of marching boots and had to lie in a ditch till they had passed. This must have been a patrol sent out to investigate the shooting. It was too dangerous to stick to the road, so I now walked the fields, well away from the road.

After some time, tired, hungry, thirsty and feeling the strain of the last few hours, I stopped in some bushes and scratched a south facing pointer in the soil. My feet were soaking so, removing my boots, I wrung my socks out into my mouth. The liquid was bitter, but helped to ease the thirst. On waking after a sound sleep, I very carefully scanned the area, but saw no sign of movement. Checking on the pointer, I set off in the direction I had marked. To my left and ahead was a dense wood which I entered and choosing a path which seemed to head south, carried on. I drank some muddy water which had collected in a rut in the path, but having lost my bread when I jumped, had to ease my hunger pangs by eating grass. Three of four hours walking brought me to a wide clearing, in the centre of which some weapon pits had been dug. While I was examining these, I heard the recognition signal and Sandy and Bryan emerged from the undergrowth.'

The other two pilots' exit from the train had been delayed, because, just as they had been about to jump, they had noticed that the train was almost at a level crossing, and knowing that these were usually guarded, they had waited until the danger was past. On hearing the two shots from down the line, they presumed that Bill had been killed or captured and started their long walk south, to the Pyrenees and Spain, without him. Sandy Dow described their reunion:

We holed up for the night in the forest, intending to revise the situation when daylight came. Dawn came soon and as we roused, we had to crouch in the undergrowth, for we heard the sound of someone approaching stealthily. A black-bereted character came gradually into sight. It was Bill, his red beret turned inside out—'To look like a peasant', he suggested, despite his Airborne smock, British army boots and equipment! This joyous reunion was almost unbelievable—that in the whole of the Ardennes Forest, he should hit the same spot that his two comrades had chosen.

To Bill Shannon, alone, hungry and deep in enemy occupied territory, this moment was one of high emotion:

I hugged the others and wept unashamedly, though our relief was nearly our undoing, for continuing our journey south and chattering non-stop, we stepped into a clearing where a German soldier was busy felling a tree. Luckily, his back was turned to us and the blows of his axe drowned the sounds of our voices. We crept silently back the way we had come and made a wide circle of the clearing. This event taught us a valuable lesson. From now on we moved in tactical bounds, taking turns at leading, the other two staying well back until the coast was clear. Thus, we hoped that if spotted, only the lead man would be caught. We weren't even sure what country we were in. The train had been heading due east, so it could have been France, Belgium, Luxembourg, or even Germany. In fact, we were in the French Ardennes, about ten kilometres west of Sedan. Because of this uncertainty, contact with civilians had to be avoided. Later that evening it started to rain heavily and as the light failed, we found a suitable bush and crept in, huddling together to keep warm.

It was still raining when we woke in the morning, but at least thirst was no problem. We were all weak from hunger and chewing grass did little to help. Resuming the journey south, with Sandy leading, we had been walking for several hours when he signalled a halt. Ahead, through the trees, we could see the outline of a massive blockhouse. Scouting cautiously nearer, we could see no doors or weapon slits facing us. After watching for several hours and seeing no movement nor hearing any sound, Sandy circled it to carry out a closer recce. He returned shortly after, grinning and calling for us to join him. What we had seen was the back of a huge concrete shrine which held a statue of the Virgin Mary, in fact, the shrine of Notre Dame de Neuvizy. To our delight, we found a torn sheet of newspaper on the floor by the altar, printed in French, which meant that we were in a potentially friendly country.

As we passed through one area of the forest we came across a patch of wild strawberries, which we collected in our berets. The trees were beginning to thin out into small fields and hedges and the rain was falling ceaselessly, so when we saw a small byre in a field we decided to seek shelter, approaching under cover of a stout hedge. The byre housed five or six cows, but we pushed in among them, the warmth of the animals bringing a little comfort to our rain-soaked bodies. Bryan was a farmer's son and he soon had his half mess tin filled with milk, which we drank with great relish. The mess tin was filled and emptied again and again. With the contents of our berets, it made the most delicious al fresco strawberries and cream! The cows had become restless, so Bryan suggested moving on before somebody came to investigate.

In the afternoon the rain stopped and as the sun was quite warm, a suitable place to dry our clothes was sought. A ploughed field seemed just right, so we stripped off our wet clothes, spreading them along the top of the ridges while we lay in the furrows. In the distance we could see military traffic passing along a road. Our joy in the warm sun was short-lived, for three girls cycled along a path near us, giggling when they saw the naked men. We dressed quickly in our soggy clothes and quit the area in case the girls raised the alarm. A mile or so further on we entered the cover of the forest again and as evening came, so did the rain and we spent another cold and miserable night.

Day three found us walking (hopefully) south. The constant rain had seeped into the sealed compass and the luminous dot on the north pointer had stuck to the underside of the glass, rendering it useless. A railway line ran across our path and a short distance away, a road crossed the line. Beside the level crossing keeper's house, stood a cherry orchard full of fruit. Skirting the house to approach the orchard unseen, we broke laden branches off the trees and retired to a railway cutting to enjoy our spoils. So engrossed were we in eating, we failed to notice the approach of a slowly moving train until it was too late to move. The train steamed past, seeming to take an age. Behind the engine was a string of trucks filled with troops going to the Front. Many sat with their legs dangling over the edge of the doors, others mounted guard, with light flak guns on flat cars. We sat open mouthed. Here we were, two hundred miles behind enemy lines, wearing camouflaged Airborne smocks and red berets, while a battalion of enemy troops passed within twenty feet of us. No shots were fired, only puzzled looks passed between the Germans. As soon as the train had disappeared round a bend we scampered back to the safety of the woods, very shaken, but still clutching our cherries.

Further on, we saw that we were nearing a tiny hamlet and it would be a good opportunity to ask for help. Bryan, who was orderly sergeant, went to an old woman who was alone, while Sandy and I watched from a distance. The results were surprising! The old woman screamed and Bryan was soon surrounded by a hostile threatening crowd. He made good his escape and we followed him.

Well into the woods, we hid in a clump of bushes, when along came a small boy, running up the path clutching a haversack. 'Messieurs! Messieurs!' he called, 'Soldats Anglais!' When it was clear that the boy was alone, we showed ourselves.

The boy said that his mother had sent him with some food and drink. Inside the bag was some bread and cheese, a piece of pork fat and a quarter of a litre of eau-de-vie. The lad apologised for the meagre rations, saying it was all they could afford. Questioned about the angry reception in the village, he said that two years ago a German had passed himself off as a British airman. His father and another man had helped the fugitive with food, clothes and money. They were arrested and shot. But, he said his mother had thought that we looked genuine. Before leaving, the ten-year-old said he wanted to be a soldier when he grew up. We stood to attention and gave him a magnificent salute, telling him that he had already proved himself to be a brave soldier. The very proud lad trotted off back to his courageous mother. Feeling that we had already had enough excitement for one day, we dined on our ambrosia and washed it down with the nectar, measured out in a half walnut shell, and settled down for the night.

The weather was dry on the fourth day and after a drink of eau-de-vie, we resumed our journey. The forest was breaking up into small copses interspersed with fields. Following one tall hedge round a field, we came to a gap and found ourselves face to face with an elderly peasant. Our first thought was to kill him, for we had now armed ourselves with stout sticks, but we decided to test him. When asked if he was a 'Bon Francais', the accepted term for a patriot, he replied that he was a true Frenchman. We explained who we were and he promised to return in half an hour with food and showed us where to wait for him. Not fully trusting him, we hid where we could keep the area under observation.

After some time a young man arrived with a milk can and a parcel. I was 'duty sergeant' and went forward first. After we had finished the food and drink the young man showed us the way to the next village and told us to call at the first house at the end of the village street, but to be discreet.

Keeping to the copses and hedges, we approached the village. As soon as the house was in sight, Sandy and Bryan went to ground and I made a wide circle to approach along the bed of a stream. After watching the house for an hour, I broke cover, climbed the bank and crossed a small bridge to the gate of the house. An elderly woman answered the door. I smiled and said in French.

'Madame, I am a British soldier, an escaped prisoner of war. Can you help me please?'
The lady smiled back, 'Get your friends and wait in the garden at the back. My sister and I saw you in the trees from our bedroom.'

Hidden under huge leaves in the back garden, we ate a delicious meal of soup, bread and cheese. We had been told that someone from the Resistance would come to see us. Later we heard the clatter of the gate and a uniformed figure came towards us with a drawn pistol. He was wearing the uniform of the hated Millice, the Vichy police, who were puppets of the Germans.'

Chapter Fourteen

Bill Shannon was sick to his heart when he saw the Millicien. All that effort for nothing! He was contemplating spending the rest of the war in a cage, when the policeman roared with laughter:

He introduced himself as a member of the Resistance and asked us lots of questions about our escape and capture. He closely examined the labels on our uniforms and boots and noted down the details of our identity discs and paybooks. He left, promising to return that evening. We were given a substantial meal and before evening the Millicien was back, grinning hugely. He said that confirmation had been received on the radio from London that we were genuine. He laughed and said, 'If not ....' and drew his finger across his throat in an unmistakeable gesture. That night we settled down in the comfort of a hay loft, fed, dry and relaxed.

In the morning we had our first wash and shave for nearly a month. Jackets and trousers were found for us, clean but full of holes and our uniforms were taken away and buried. After a good breakfast, we left our hosts, the sisters Quentin, thanking them warmly and followed our two guides, who had come to Auboncourt for us. We had been instructed, that in the event of anyone speaking to us, we were only to say 'Polski', as there were many Polish workers in the area in equally tatty clothes. Our guides led us through Amagne-Lucquy, where a train had been derailed the night before. We had to pass close by a scene where a group of Russian POWs were re-railing the wagons under the control of armed guards. As we passed, one of a group of spectators came over to us with a cigarette in his mouth and asked for a light. Horrified, we shook our heads saying 'Polski, Polski'. The man shrugged and turned away, but we felt that he was suspicious.

At the next village, Amagne, which seemed deserted, we were led into a bar where we were obviously expected. Glasses and bottles awaited us on a table and a small group pressed forward, eager to shake our hands.

Well refreshed, we resumed our journey along a quiet track which brought us to a wide river. The guides said that this was the Aisnes, and that we would ford it. We had no difficulty as the current was not strong and the water level was below our thighs. On reaching the far bank, the two Frenchmen introduced our new guide, a pretty teenage girl sitting on a bike. Farewells were made and the two Frenchmen returned across the river. The girl rode slowly about fifty yards ahead, her white dress making it easy to follow her among the trees and hedges.

After walking for several hours we saw a village in the distance. When we got nearer, our guide left the track and walked across the fields to a high wall which contained many gates. She entered one and, ensuring that there was no-one about, beckoned us to join her quickly. A friendly reception awaited us. Jean Deguerne, farmer, Resistance Chief and one-time Capitaine in the Chasseurs d'Alpins, his wife Marthe, his eldest daughter Jeanne, the guide Reine, his youngest Eliane, his father-in-law Grandpère, René a former French artilleryman and George, an American airgunner, who had bailed out of a B-17.

Jean and his family were full of fun and laughed at the 'scare-crows', taking a photograph of them. Fresh clothes were found and our shirts and underclothes washed. We finally felt human again! We shared a comfortable bedroom overlooking the farmyard. The farmhouse was terraced, standing in a street of similar houses in the village of Ville-sur-Retoume. Behind the house was a long yard, flanked on one side by small storerooms, an earth privy and a manure dump. On the other side were small pens for pigs and geese, a cow shed, a stable and a barn. In one of the storage rooms, Jean kept his arms, ammunition and explosives in a pig-swill boiler.

During our stay, Jean's group received a drop of new supplies which were brought into the yard, still in their container. We assisted in the degreasing, cleaning and stowing of the precious cargo. I had served in a mounted Yeomanry regiment before the War and looked after Jean's horse when it was brought in from the fields and the others helped in general work around the yard, though only René was able to go out. On 14 July, France's National Day, someone unknown had hung the proscribed tricolour on the village war memorial. Although there weren't any Germans in the village, a motorised patrol passed through several times a day. The morning patrol saw the flag and returned with reinforcements. Hostages were taken from the village and the German commander told the Mayor that unless the culprit gave himself up by evening, the hostages would be shot.

Grandpère, who had been a refugee as a boy in the Franco-Prussian War, again in the First World War and once more in 1940, when he was wounded in the strafing, said he would go forward and claim responsibility for the flag. The family tried to dissuade him, but to no avail. That evening he went to meet the German commander, the hostages were released and Grandpère taken away for interrogation. Jean announced that we must all leave early the next morning. Members of the group arrived at night to remove all the sabotage materials and documents for distribution to safe houses and the British and the American left with a guide. Robert, Jean and the girls went in another direction leaving Marthe Deguerne alone. Later that morning, she too was arrested, finally ending up in Buchenwald.

Our route lay almost completely across country for about seven miles to the village of Tagnon, on the busy N51 route to Belgium. In a bar in the main street we met our new guardian, Pierre Toufflin, local stationmaster and Chef de Resistance. After an anisette we were taken to the house of Pierre's mother, who was ill in hospital. As the house was supposed to be unoccupied, the shutters had to be kept closed at the front, but we were free to go out into the walled garden at the back. Later, another American airman was brought in to join us. The five of us had to share one bed in a ground floor room which was very hot, but everyone was in good humour. A young man used to bring a basket of food and drink for us every day. On most nights, German lorries used to pull up on the verge under the window and we could hear the conversation of the occupants through the open windows, but could not understand what was being said.

One hot day when we were sitting in the sun in the garden, a small boy climbed the wall to scrump fruit from the garden. When he saw us, he ran off shouting 'Assassins! Terroristes!' at the top of his voice. Events moved swiftly. A small truck loaded with barrels was reversed into the covered yard alongside the house. Pierre Toufflin jumped out, made a space among the barrels and waved us in. He and Robert placed empty barrels over to cover us. I was able to see through a gap in the side of the truck and as we neared the crossroads at Bergincourt, Pierre sounded his horn furiously in true Gallic fashion. A German Military Policeman on duty at the junction waved him through. Two miles further on, I saw two truckloads of troops speeding to Tagnon to deal with the 'terrorists'.

There was a short stop outside a horse-butcher's shop where steak sandwiches were passed through the side of the truck to the pilots, before the journey continued. The next place of refuge was a cafe, which was half-cafe, half-brothel.

The truck entered a built-up area and stopped at a cafe. We were helped out and shown into a back room, where a hard-faced Madame and some of her girls were seated at a large table. When we were all settled a couple of bottles of champagne were opened and toasts drunk. In the middle of this, the door opened and a young German soldier came into the room. I noticed that Robert, who was sitting beside me, had his automatic out, covering the soldier. The German broke the awkward silence by asking for some chalk for his billiard cue! The drinks finished, we were shown upstairs to relax while new homes were found for us. We were packed into a truck once more and taken to the enclosed yard of a gymnasium. Everyone dismounted to more handshakes and more champagne and we were told that we were now in the city of Rheims and that we would have to be split up.'

Sandy Dow, 'Lucky' Whetstone, an American fighter pilot and Larry Stein, an American Fortress pilot, were all billeted with a widow in her sixties, Mme. André, who lived at 67 Rue Camille Lenoir, just round the corner from Rheims Cathedral. Sandy Dow continued to be full of admiration for the courage and hospitality this old woman showed the three pilots:

Mme. Andre was proud of her not unreasonable English, but into almost every English sentence, she seemed to introduce, as if it were some kind of incantation, the phrase 'Les sales Boches', sometimes spitting with the utterance and, even more so, if she happened to look out of her upstairs window and see any German soldiers as they, not infrequently, passed by.

Meals, simple as they had to be, were always elegantly served in the dining room while she, as hostess, sat in the kitchen. She often got up at six in the morning to go out into the woods to try to trap a rabbit to augment the meagre rations. Her soups were delicious, her good humour unbounded and her pride, swollen with her joy of caring for the enemies of 'les sales Boches', added to her great dignity.

Sandy and the two Americans also spent some time in the home of another family in Rheims area, the Vandecosteeles. '*Groupe Bourlon*', the Resistance group in the city, were very busy in the summer of 1944, sheltering somewhere between one hundred and fifty and two hundred Allied servicemen, especially as at no time, did the group consist of more than a dozen active members. Not only were they running an escape route, but they were also active in sabotaging the German war machine. Bill Shannon's next haven was another cafe, the 'Á la Grappe', in Rue Ernest Renan on the banks of the canal:

My guardienne was a striking widow, Mme. Jeanne Vallois, in her mid-forties, her daughter Gilberte and son-in-law René. This was only to be a temporary stop, my ultimate destination was to be the home of a baker, which was near the liquid air factory, sabotaged a couple of nights earlier by the Resistance. As the area was still swarming with police and troops it was unsafe to venture near. The Groupe Bourlon, who had blown up the factory, used to gather in the back room of the cafe each night. One night, they brought a new man in with them who wanted to meet me. He introduced himself as a liaison officer for a Canadian agent, who was based in the Forêt de Champagne. This agent wanted to question me and said he would send a car for me three days from then. At four o'clock the next morning, the Gestapo arrived at the baker's house and he was shot dead as he tried to escape. The Groupe held an immediate enquiry to find the traitor. I was exonerated as I had not left the cafe, but the liaison officer was the obvious suspect. He was lured into the forest on some pretext and there tortured. He confessed to working for the Gestapo, was executed and buried without trace.

The Groupe had to move me at once, for it was not known if my whereabouts were already known to the Gestapo HQ in Rue Jeanne d'Arc. I was taken to the home of Guy Tabary, one of the younger members of the Groupe. Guy lived with his father, Artur, a retired police sergeant-major, and his mother in the Rue de Courselles, on the outskirts of the town. Guy had been an airgunner in the French Air Force. After 1940, he went to the south-east and joined the Maquis in the mountains. The Tabary family were poor, for Artur's pension had not been paid under the German occupation and Guy could not work because officially, he was not in Rheims. The Resistance helped by making payments to such people and by giving parcels of food. On one occasion I dined on wild boar, but usually the fare was very basic.

The end of Tabary's garden backed on to a German barracks and I often walked down to the party wall when the light had faded, to listen to the troops singing, which they did very well. One favourite, of theirs and mine, was Lili Marlene. However, there was no escape route from that house in the event of a raid, except over that wall! Curfew was from 9 p.m. to 6 a.m. Anyone out on the streets between these times without a special pass could be arrested or shot out of hand. Guy went out on his bike on many nights, automatic pistol in his belt, and wire cutters in his pocket. His forté was interfering with communications, but of course he also took part in Groupe sabotage missions, such as the liquid air factory. One evening, a police inspector, who was a friend of the family, called. He had bad news. The house was to be raided that night. Someone had reported seeing Guy and the police were coming to search for him. When the inspector, who was also a member of Groupe Bourlon, left, Artur insisted that everyone sat at the table and ate a full meal. They had hidden anything which might suggest that there were any occupants of the house other than the old couple.

Mme. Jeanne Vallois, who was to be the front guide, arrived with a spare cycle. I was to ride about thirty metres behind her, while Guy rode a similar distance behind as guard. Speed was essential as curfew was near and our route lay across the city. As we approached the Pont du Laon, the chain came off my bike, right beside a Millicien, who was talking to another man. While Guy stopped to light a cigarette, I fumbled, with shaking hands, to fix the chain. Jeanne's white dress was seen and the journey resumed through nearly deserted streets. The new house was an apartment over a shop on the busy Avenue Jean-Jaures, the main route from Paris to Brussels. The curfew was down by the time that Jeanne and Guy handed me over and they had to return by a perilous route, dodging patrols. Artur Tabary and his wife were arrested. Artur, aged eighty, was so badly beaten that he became deaf

I was pleased to find myself in the same house as Bryan Helme, for it was a relief to be able to talk English again. Also hidden there, was an American Lieutenant, Adam Hunt, who had bailed out of a stricken P38. The family who owned the house were charming people. Max Herbé, jeweller and watchmaker, had served in the 1914–18 War and in the Maginot line in 1939–40. His wife, Lydie, came from Strasbourg in Alsace and was a fervent patriot, though she spoke French with a heavy German accent. Alsace had been under German domination from 1870 to 1918 and the French language had been forbidden. As a girl in the First World War, she had been made to work in a quarry and her hatred of the Germans was absolute. Their son was away in the French Navy, but their two daughters, Janine aged nineteen and Danielle aged seventeen, were at home. The living quarters were on the first floor above the jeweller's shop. Another apartment on the same floor shared the stairs and the street door. The standard of living at the Herbé's was higher than in other places that we had stayed in, but it cost Max a lot of money on the black market to maintain this standard. Mme. Herbé was a superb cook and produced some wonderful meals. Especially memorable were her cherry tarts laced with kirsch.

We had a happy time reading, playing cards, listening to AFN on the radio and flirting with the girls. One day there was a cloudburst which lasted for hours, flooding shops and houses and cafe tables and chairs floated away down the street. When the water had subsided, we and the girls went down into the shop to mop up and clean away the mud. As we worked, a German soldier entered the shop and, completely ignoring the workers, asked about a watch repair. When he had gone Max joked that the Boche had just missed a chance of leave and promotion. On another occasion two German soldiers entered the living room, without warning, when we were listening to AFN, our backs to the door. Lydie Herbé, fortunately, was close by and took charge of the situation. She ranted and raved at the two Boche.

'How dare you break into the home of a good Hausfrau. I will report you to your commanding officer....' The two soldiers turned and fled. It seemed that they had been looking for cycles. The summer was very hot and the windows were always wide open. Often army lorries would stop outside the windows and Lydie would lean over the balcony, her gold blonde hair done up in plaits and looking a typical frau. She would talk sympathetically to the troops below and they would give her all the latest news from the Front. The wounded looked pathetic as they lay in open trucks, their paper bandages soaked with blood and in their eyes, a haunted look, for it was a nerve-wracking experience to move on the roads at day, when the Allies had complete command of the air.

One evening, Max agreed to take the three airmen for a walk to see Rheims Cathedral. The first part of the walk took us to the house of Edgard Petibon, the horse-butcher who had passed us those marvellous sandwiches when we first entered Rheims. After walking round the Cathedral and admiring its construction, we set off for home. As we entered the Place Aristide Briande, following Max at a distance, an army lorry turned onto the square, a feldwebel standing on the running board. I was slightly ahead of the other two pilots and the truck stopped right beside me. The feldwebel asked for the Place Royale, and not wanting to risk my French in case the German was a good French speaker, I pointed to my mouth and ears and shook my head. The feldwebel became very angry and shook me by the shoulders, cursing me. Max hurried back and gave the man the instructions he needed, but after that we all felt that it would be unwise to venture out into the city again.

As the Allies approached the Seine, the Germans were getting more jumpy and their controls became stricter. Word was received that two evading airmen had been captured in the home of Charles Mutot, a friend of Guy. Charles had been able to jump out of the window and escape, although he was shot in the leg. The two airmen had been taken to the Rue Jeanne d'Arc and tortured. One, a Canadian named Ralph, broke under the torture and revealed names and addresses. Many members of the Resistance were arrested and the two airmen were shot by the Gestapo. At 4 a.m. one morning, the Herbé family were awakened by the sound of police sirens and several cars pulled up outside the door. They heard the street door burst open and the thud of boots on the stairs. By now everyone was up and dressed and waiting full of apprehension. To everyone's great relief the raid was on the unfortunate family across the landing. To shouts and screams, the man of the house was led away and never seen again. The family never learned his fate.

The American lieutenant was very immature and liked to play the childish game of standing near the window and pointing his fingers, pretending to shoot German soldiers passing in the street below. Mme. Herbé was very worried about this behaviour and she tried several times to warn him about it, but she could not get through to him. In despair she turned to me, who was the eldest of the trio. I tackled Hunt in a forthright manner, pointing out the possible consequences of his stupid conduct. Hunt resented being told off by a sergeant and sulked for days after. In fact, two days before the Liberation, a family across the road had denounced the Herbés to the Gestapo, for they had seen someone at the window who was not a member of the family. Thankfully, the Gestapo were too busy destroying evidence and saving their own skins to worry about any new cases.

With great joy the fall of Paris was celebrated and everyone knew that the turn of Rheims would not be too long. Around this time I developed dysentery, a very embarrassing and distressing disease in a closed community. A bed was made up for me next to the toilet door, but even this was too far sometimes. Max realised that he would have to get a doctor to see me, but it was difficult in the circumstances. A plan was adopted—Danielle was to arrive on her bicycle, hit the kerb outside the shop and fall off, screaming and crying on the floor. Mother would rush out of the shop and weep at her poor daughter and father would carry Danielle upstairs while Janine would go off on her bicycle to fetch the doctor. It all worked perfectly, the doctor treated me with opium and I was back on my feet within the week.

For some days before the Liberation, the non-essential German personnel had been making their way north to Belgium or north-east to Germany. All kinds of rickety transport was pressed into service. There were several military hospitals in Rheims and they evacuated all but their most seriously wounded. Depots and barracks closed down and it was a time of great tension and danger. Troops roamed around looting and searching for cycles and civilian clothing, even though the firing squad awaited any caught out of uniform. The Herbés closed their shop and all the valuables were brought upstairs. One evening, loud-speaker vans toured the city warning that any civilian found on the streets or seen at a window would be shot. We knew that the Allies must be close. Patrols roamed the streets, looking apprehensively all around and the rattle of small arms fire and the occasional crump of grenades could be heard through the night. By the morning of 30th August all was unnaturally quiet, then a policeman rode into the square.

'They're here!' he shouted. 'The Americans are here!' Doors and shutters were flung open and people erupted onto the streets. As I stood at the corner of Avenue Jean-Jaures, a wary GI poked his rifle, and then his head, round the corner.

'It's okay,' I greeted him. 'They've all buggered off!

'You speak good English!' said the Gl.

So I should,' I replied. 'I'm a British POW. Welcome to Rheims.'

After breakfast, a friend of the Herbés, Edouard l'Amiable, who used to work for Pommery and Grenoi, called. He insisted that the first task for us must be to liberate Pommery's caves. We were received with great acclaim by management and workers alike, a line was drawn in the visitors' book and we were asked to start a fresh page as liberators. Needless to say, the best vintage Champagne flowed freely and we were shown round the famous caves and the processes explained to us. On leaving, we were given bottles of Champagne and souvenir postcard packs. Lieutenant Hunt left the family to join an American officers' mess, but the next day he returned with American uniforms for Bryan and myself, complete with combat jacket and moulded helmet liner.

On the 2 September, I was asked to go round to the various safe houses and inform the other forty-two escapers and evaders hidden there, to assemble the next morning for the trip to Paris.

I was given a jeep and a driver and Jeanine Mutot came along as guide. We were stopped in one street by a crowd, who informed us that there were six German soldiers hiding in a house and would we flush them out? As neither myself nor the driver was armed, we could only report the location to the next troops we met. After the Liberation came the retribution. Gangs roamed the streets looking for collaborators, real or imagined, and many personal scores were settled. The most vociferous of those seeking reprisals were, as always, those who had taken little or no part in the Resistance. One gang stopped outside the Herbés' shop, which was still shuttered, shouting that Mme. Herbé was German and that she had helped the Boches. She brought Bryan and myself to the window and told the crowd that she had sheltered us. We backed her and told the crowd to clear off, or words to that effect!

On 3rd September, the escapers and evaders assembled in the yard of Heideck & Cie. We were loaded into a convoy of GS trucks, which already contained hundreds of German POW's, most in uniform, but some in civilian clothes. Armed guards, mostly Black, rode in the trucks and thus began the one hundred mile trip to Paris, through devastated towns, bumping across Bailey bridges and cratered roads. At Fontainebleau everyone was marched into a huge POW cage, irrespective of dress or nationality. After a few hours and a meal, the new arrivals were questioned and the Allies separated. Later, we were driven to the

Hotel Maurice, Rue de Rivoli in Paris. This was the HQ of USCIC, and was the only hotel in Paris with electric light at that time. Bullet holes, blood stains and smashed mirrors showed some signs of the bitter struggle that had taken place here ten days before. This had been the HQ of Colonel-General Von Choltitz, Military Governor of Paris. The meals caused some amusement, for they were served in the grand dining room by the original white-coated staff, who served the biscuits of the K-Rations with silver tongs from silver salvers, with all the decorum of a state banquet.

The three glider pilots were interrogated by a Squadron Leader from the RAF and I was asked to write down an account of our escape and subsequent evasion. About six months later, I attended a lecture on escape and evasion at Fargo Camp, and the lecturer read out my account word for word! On 5th September, the British element was driven to Orly Airport, which at the time only had tented accommodation, and we were flown to Hendon in a C-47 of the USAAF and driven on to the Great Central Hotel in the Marylebone Road, the London HQ of MI9. We were each shown to separate rooms and after I had settled in I decided to go and have a chat with Sandy and Bryan. An armed sentry on the corridor stopped me and ordered me to stay in my room until I had been interrogated. During the interrogation the next day, I was surprised to learn that the three of us had been kept under surveillance by London and our every move updated on a map. The interrogation officer explained, with a grin, that all those adrift weren't equally keen on returning and those who tried to remain in France were in for a shock when hostilities ceased. The next day we were kitted out with new uniforms, given leave passes for five weeks with double ration tickets, and warrants for travel home.

At the end of our leave we had to report to No. 1 Centre at Matlock Bath, which was a psychiatric unit, full of soldiers trying to get out of the army, except for sixty Airborne troops, including Bill Musitano from 'D' Squadron, all of whom were agitating to be returned to their parent units. In the end we made such a nuisance of ourselves that the authorities gave way and all sixty were posted back to the Airborne forces. The four of us returned to 'D' Squadron in early November, at the new location of Wethersfield in Essex. We were shattered when we realised how many of our friends had not returned from Normandy and Arnhem. In my hut, of the original twenty-two, only two remained!'

The three pilots, who owed so much to *Groupe Bourlon* never forgot their debt. They returned a number of times after the War and corresponded regularly at Christmas time. Mmes. Jeanne Vallois and Lydie Herbé both lived into their nineties. The former remained a force to be reckoned with, her steely character dominating any room.

The risk that these brave French men and women took every day of the occupation cannot be overstated. Had they been caught, they and their families would have been tortured and shot, or sent to the concentration camps—a fate that befell many. Lydie Herbé still shuddered at the memory of the constant fear, that this might have become reality for her and her two teenage daughters in 1944, yet she would have done it all again if France asked. Of Mme. André, there is a sad conclusion, to the story. At New Year in 1960, instead of a card, Sandy Dow received a poignant letter telling him that she had been knocked down by a tourist coach, suffered a fractured pelvis and died in hospital from pneumonia. The coach had been British and the driver had been more concerned about the disruption to his schedule, than the old lady—a sad tale indeed.

Some years after the War, the Gestapo personnel from Rheims, were tracked down and executed for the many murders they had committed in the area. The French paratroops, whom the glider pilots had befriended on the train were never listed as POW. They had, as they had feared, been executed for booby-trapping their equipment before capture.

Chapter Fifteen

The first question any book concerned with a military operation must ask in conclusion is, 'Was the operation a success?' There have been several opinions on the success of 'Tonga' from various sources. One school of thought looks on the operation as a costly failure and a waste of good lives; another sees it as a complete success. The probable truth is somewhere in between. The first criticism is really about the need for the operation in the first place. It is easy, with hindsight, to criticise planners for bad judgement, as historians have the advantage of access to far superior military intelligence than the commanders of the day ever had, and the complexity of D-Day planning almost defies belief at times. If one looks at the information available to the planners at the time, then there is no doubt, that to have landed without the 'insurance' which *Tonga* offered, would have been foolhardy. Perhaps the key to answering the question of success is to study whether or not the aims of the operation were met. All the tasks given to the Airborne troops were carried out. On these criteria alone, *Tonga* must be viewed as successful. Not everything went to plan—far from it. Many gliders and parachutists landed well away from their targets and much equipment went astray. The casualties on some tasks were horrendous, yet the jobs were still done.

The 5th Parachute Brigade Group's tasks were all carried out. The bridges over the Orne River and Caen Canal were taken intact and held until the Airborne element was relieved by the seaborne forces. Without control of these bridges, the invasion could have been contained in a small beach-head and, at the best, casualties would have been far higher or, at the worst, the invasion repulsed. The area of LZ 'N' was cleared and held, on schedule. Perhaps the part of the operation that went the most wrong was the seizure of the Merville Battery, yet this too was accomplished. The guns of Merville, although smaller than Intelligence suggested, were put out of action and were unable to bombard the beach-head. The 9th Parachute Battalion suffered appalling casualties in taking the Battery and carrying out their other tasks, virtually ceasing to exist as a viable military unit until heavily reinforced.

The bridges over the Dives and Divette were blown and the German armour denied this eastern access to the beach-head. Although this part of the operation was badly affected, when much of the supplies and troops landed in the wrong place, 'Airborne attitude' saved the day. After the bridges had been destroyed, the troops held the area until relieved by 1st Special Service Brigade, as planned.

The anti-tank screen was put in place in the Ranville area and proved to be effective against a number of armoured German counter-attacks, the accompanying infantry being dealt with by the Airborne soldiers, dug in alongside the guns. Had the Germans used heavier tanks, then it might have been a different story, but any speculation on this point is just useless conjecture. The massed glider landings of *Mallard* reinforced the 6th Airborne's hold on the area to the point where it would have taken more than the Germans had in the immediate area to shift them. Once this stage had been reached, then nothing could stop the break-out from the beach-head. *Tonga* made all this possible.

The major problem that the Glider Pilots faced was finding the LZs. This was due, as is discussed in an earlier chapter, to a combination of badly prepared equipment, navigational errors by some of the RAF crews, who dropped the Pathfinders or towed the gliders, and poor visibility on the night, though it should be stressed that many of the tug pilots went to extraordinary lengths to release their gliders in the correct position. Had the Rebecca-Eureka beacons been placed accurately, then many more gliders would have reached the correct landing areas. The decision to bomb Merville, so soon before the gliders were due to land, was also probably flawed, as this was directly responsible for several crucial gliders losing their bearings in the dust and smoke thrown up by the explosions. A sound scattering of smaller anti-personnel bombs, to detonate the mines and inconvenience the garrison, would have served the paratroops better. Low cloud also served to hinder the gliders and tugs, the turbulent air and zero visibility in the cloud being responsible for many a broken tow-rope. This, however, was a potential hazard for any glider operation, and beyond the control of the D-Day planners.

The actual performance of the equipment varied. The unloading procedure in combat of the Horsa Mk.I, was patently unsatisfactory. The delays, or even in some cases the impossibility, of removing the tail to unload the contents of the glider, hazarded the success of the mission. This problem had obvious been recognised in certain quarters before D-Day, as the Horsa Mk.II was beginning to be built. However, the allocation of the later mark seems to have been a lottery, with little planning. It was a pity that certain strategically important gliders were not of the later type, which were not on general issue until after Arnhem, four months later. Lieutenant-Colonel Murray commented favourably on the white identification stripes on the wings of the gliders, in his post-operation report to Colonel Chatterton. (WOl71/1283 174049) These 'were of great value for picking out gliders already landed. If these markings are dispensed with in the future, something of the same nature on upper surfaces of the wings is most desirable.' He also remarked on the need for better differential brakes to be fitted to the gliders if they had to land on obstructed LZs on any future operation. This would allow the pilots a greater degree of steering once on the ground.

The actual employment of the glider pilots on the ground was also commented on by both Major Royle and Major Griffith who were both of the opinion that more use could have been made of the pilots in a defensive role on the LZs. John Royle suggested that his men were ideally suited for the task of sniper hunting. To help in this task he suggested a revision of the personal weapon scales, so that each section included two trained snipers with Lee Enfield No. 4 'T' rifles and two men with Sten Mk.V sub-machine-guns in place of rifles.

The problem of German snipers was probably over-rated by Major Royle. It is common for soldiers to attribute all 'effective fire' to snipers. 'Effective fire' is defined as shots which strike the target, or force the troops to take immediate cover. He reported that at 1025 hours on 6 June, 'three men wounded, one fatally, by a burst of fire from South—cause unknown, but suspected snipers with 9mm sub-machine-gun.' This was almost certainly just an unlucky burst of fire. Snipers do not use a gun with which accurate shooting, at any range above fifty metres is a matter of luck. Neither, do snipers fire in 'bursts'. A good sniper fires one round from a telescopic sighted rifle and hits the target at medium to long range. While there can be no doubt that there were snipers at work in the immediate area of LZ 'N', much of the problem was simply aimed shots from ordinary infantrymen, or some of the many shots fired in the general direction of the LZ striking home.

After Normandy, came Arnhem, followed by the crossing of the Rhine. Twenty-four of those pilots who had survived the rigours of *Tonga* died on these two operations and many more were wounded or captured, yet the survivors still flew. Had it not been for the surrender of Japan, after the bombing of Hiroshima and Nagasaki, then some of them would have flown Wacos in the proposed invasion of Japan. The spirit, which prompted them to volunteer for this most hazardous of wartime occupations, was evident after demobilisation. Glider Pilots took up the challenge of peacetime occupations with equal verve. Many became successful lawyers, surgeons, teachers, artists, businessmen, actors or policemen, but two factors seem to unite them all, and they are, a common belief in the humanity of mankind and a knowledge that war is a criminal waste of virile, young lives. Chatterton's Total Soldiers became 'Total Civilians'.

Appendix One

Comments on Tonga Gliders

† = KIA (Tonga)   * = POW ‡ = KIA (Arnhem & the Rhine)

Wave One: Tarrant Rushton under command of 'B' Sqn (Towed by Halifaxes from 298 & 644 Sqns)
LZ 'X' = Caen Canal Bridge LZ 'Y' = Orne River Bridge
Loads:
Reinforced company of 2nd Bn. OBLI with RE. attached.
CN 91: Maj. R. J. Howard Lt H.D. Brotheridge 25 Platoon, D Coy.
CN 92: Lt D. J. Wood 24 Platoon, D Coy.
CN 93: Lt R. A. A. Smith 14 Platoon, B Coy.
CN 94: Capt. B. C. E. Priday (2IC) Lt C. A. Hooper 22 Platoon, D Coy.
CN 95: Lt E. J. Sweeney 23 Platoon, D Coy.
CN 96: Lt D. B. Fox 17 Platoon, B Coy.

CN.	LZ.	Glider Pilots		Comments
91	X	S/Sgt Wallwork, J.	S/Sgt Ainsworth, J	Landed on LZ.
92	X	S/Sgt Boland, O.	Sgt Hobbs, B.	Landed on LZ.
93	X	S/Sgt Barkway, G.	Sgt Boyle, P.	Landed on LZ.
94	Y	‡S/Sgt Lawrence, A.	S/Sgt Shorter, H.	Landed on LZ.
95	Y	S/Sgt Pearson, S.	S/Sgt Guthrie, L.	Landed at Dives Bridge, 20 miles from LZ.
96	Y	S/Sgt Howard, R.	S/Sgt Baacke, F.	Landed on LZ.

Wave Two: Blakehill Farm 'F' Sqn
(Towed by Dakotas of 233 Sqn)
Loads CN 218–222: heavy weapons from 8th Parachute Bn. (Jeeps and explosives to blow Diver River bridges).
CN 223: 224 Parachute Field Ambulance RAMC

CN.	LZ.	Glider Pilots		Comments
218	K	Lt Pickwoad, A. E.	Sgt Watts, M.	Landed on LZ.
219	K	S/Sgt Banks, R.	Sgt Hebblethwaite, B.	Landed on LZ.
220	K	*S/Sgt Ridgeway, W.	†Sgt Foster, P.	Landed in marsh nr Vimont. Ridgeway captured. Foster shot whilst attempting to get to Allied lines
221	K	S/Sgt England, W.	Sgt Graham, J.	Landed LZ N. England wounded and captured. Freed by Para patrol.
222	K	S/Sgt Heron, J.	Sgt Davidson, D.	Landed on LZ N.
223	K	S/Sgt Weeden, L.	Sgt Griffiths, S.	Landed on LZ N.

Wave Two: Down Ampney 'E' Sqn
(Towed by Dakotas of 271 Sqn)
(Allocation for CN 261, 262, 265, 266, 277 known. Rest presumed)
Loads:
CN 261–262: HQ 3rd Parachute Bde.
CN 263–265: 1 (Canadian) Parachute Bn.
CN 266–267: 4 A/L Anti-Tank Bty.

CN.	LZ.	Glider Pilots		Comments
261	V	Lt Dodwell, C. B.	*Sgt Osborne, B.	Osborne injured on landing 2 miles short of LZ.
262	V	S/Sgt Andrews, N. (DFM)	Sgt Senier, P.	Landed on 'an' LZ.
263	V	S/Sgt Lovett, J.	Sgt Wilson, J. L.	Landed on LZ.
264	V	*S/Sgt Gardner, A.	*Sgt Oliver, A.	Landed in Dives Valley nr. Briqueville in 3 feet of water (1.5 miles S of LZ V).
265	V	S/Sgt Rancom, H.	*Sgt Collard, E.	Landed in minefield. Hid up for a few days and made for Paris. Captured *en route* by the SS. Rancom's arm amputated.
266	V	S/Sgt Herbert, W.	Sgt Moorcraft, G.	Landed NE of Bures-sur-Dives.
267	V	†S/Sgt Saunders, V.	†Sgt Fuell, J.	Came down 7 miles SE of LZ V. Crew killed in landing.

Wave Two: Harwell 'A' Sqn
(Towed by Albemarles of 295 & 570 Sqns)
Loads:
CN 66–68: 9th Parachute Bn.
CN 69: No. 3 Section 224 Parachute Field Ambulance RAMC

CN.	LZ.	Glider Pilots		Comments
66	V	†S/Sgt Ockwell, V.	*Sgt Hellyer, T. R.	Hit pole on landing, Ockwell killed.
67	V	†S/Sgt Marfleet, W. K.	†Sgt Haines, V.	All on board drowned when glider crashed off Normandy coast.
68	V	S/Sgt Thorpe, E.	Sgt Hardie, R.	Landed 7.5 miles SW of LZ. Hardie badly injured when glider hit tree.
69	V	S/Sgt Bramah, M.	Sgt Bartley, R.	Crashed in woods nr Villers-sur-Mer.

Wave Three: Brize Norton 'B' Sqn
(Towed by Albemarles of 296 Sqn)
(Allocation known)
Loads:
CN 27-28A: *Coup de Main Party and explosives for assault on Merville Battery by 9th Parachute Bn.*
CN 27: *Lt H. Pond & 21men of A Coy, 9th Parachute Bn./591 Para Sqn RE.*
CN 28: Capt. R. Gordon-Brown & 21 men of A Coy, 9th Parachute Bn./591 Para Sqn RE.
CN 28A: Lt H. Smythe & 21 men of A Coy, 9th Parachute Bn./591 Para Sqn RE.
CN 29–36: 5th Parachute Bde.
CN 37–44: RE (41-43 carried bulldozers)
CN 45: FOO 5th Parachute Bde.

CN.	LZ.	Glider Pilots		Comments
27	Battery	‡S/Sgt Kerr, D.	‡S/Sgt Walker, H.	Prem release, landed in orchard nr BTY.
28	Battery	S/Sgt Bone, S.	Sgt Dean, L.	Prem release, landing OK
28A	Battery	S/Sgt Baldwin, A.	Sgt Michie J.	Tow-rope broke, landed in UK.
29	N	S/Sgt Bowen, J.	‡Capt. Smellie, J.	Landed on LZ.
30	N	S/Sgt Jenkins, N.	Sgt Raspison, E.	Landed on LZ.
31	N	S/Sgt Nye, G.	Sgt Smith, A.	Landed on LZ.
32	N	*‡S/Sgt Harris, H.	†Sgt Nash, J.	Landed on LZ.

33	N	S/Sgt Startup, F.	Sgt Worthington, L.	Landed on LZ.
34	N	S/Sgt Apps, W.	‡Sgt Briggs, G.	Landed on LZ.
35	N	†S/Sgt Hopgood, C.	†Sgt Phillips, D.	Killed on landing.
36	N	S/Sgt Hedgecock, L.	Sgt Jackson, C.	Landed on LZ.
37	N	S/Sgt Shepherd, A.	Sgt Bullivant, L.	Returned to base. Aileron trouble.
38	N	S/Sgt Corry, F.	Sgt Wright, R.	Prem release, landed on school sports field in Ranville.
39	N	S/Sgt Goodwin, B.	†Sgt Beveridge, H.	Hit pole. Beveridge killed. Load OK.
40	N	‡Lt. Norton, H. M. R.	Sgt Waterhouse, C.	Prem release, landed on LZ.
41	N	S/Sgt Evans, K. A.	Sgt Thompson, J.	On landing Evans injured, Thompson wounded.
42	N	†S/Sgt Brabham, J.	†Sgt Lightowler, E.	Drowned when glider came down off coast.
43	N	S/Sgt Ashby, R.	Sgt Donaldson, J.	Landed on LZ.
44	N	S/Sgt Steele, R.	‡Sgt Greene, J.	Landed on LZ.
45	N	*S/Sgt Jones, W.	*Sgt Potts, D. J.	Landed well off LZ. Potts wounded by flak.

Wave Three: Harwell 'A' Sqn & R.H.Q.
(Towed by Albemarles of 295 and 570 Sqns)
(Allocation known)
Loads:
CN 70–89: 6th Airborne Div HQ
CN 90: FOO 5th Parachute Bde.

CN.	LZ.	Glider Pilots		Comments
70	N	Maj. Griffith, S. C.	SSM. Mew, K.	Passenger – Maj. Gen. R. Gale .
71	N	‡Maj. Royle, J. P.	Lt. Smith. S. R.	Tow-rope broke. Force landed in minefield 4 miles E of LZ.
72	N	†S/Sgt Stear, A.	Sgt Wilson, J.	Hit farm building on landing.
73	N	2Lt Fletcher, P. N.	Sgt Sheills. G.	Landed on LZ.
74	N	†S/Sgt Wright, D.	†Sgt Powell, B.	Powell killed in landing at Château de Grangues, Wright shot by Germans after alleged escape attempt.

75	N	S/Sgt Edwards, J. R.	‡Sgt Ferguson, W. S.	Landed on LZ.
76	N	S/Sgt Westerby, K.	Sgt Warren, W.	Landed on LZ.
77	N	*S/Sgt Rushton. D.	*Sgt Phillips. P.	Landed on LZ.
78	N	S/Sgt Bradshaw, W.	Lt. Chapman, H. K.	Landed on LZ.
79	N	S/Sgt Wilson, P. J.	‡Sgt Harris, H.	Came down in sea off Worthing.
80	N	T/Capt. Cross, R. K.	S/Sgt Bishop, C.	Landed on LZ.
81	N	S/Sgt Rennison, C.	Sgt Snowdon, J.	Landed on LZ.
82	N	†S/Sgt Luff. R.	†Lt. Bromley, J. L.	Hit tree at Château de Grangues.
83	N	S/Sgt Hannan, K.	Sgt Spencer, B.	Landed on LZ.
84	N	*S/Sgt Hunter, A.	*Sgt Collins, C.	Hit by flak. Made landfall. All on board taken prisoner.
85	N	S/Sgt Creed, R.	†Sgt Rigg., A.	Hit another glider on landing. Rigg killed.
86	N	S/Sgt Kirkham, K.	S/Sgt Smeaton, R. J.	Landed on LZ.
87	N	S/Sgt Kirkman, L.	Sgt Laycock. C.	Came down in sea off Worthing.
88	N	S/Sgt Houghton. D.	Sgt Tincombe. D.	Landed on LZ.
89	N	Lt-Col. Murray, I. A	Capt. Bottomley, J. B.	Passengers—Brigadier the Hon. Hugh Kindersley and War Correspondent Chester Wilmot. Landed on LZ.
90	N	S/Sgt Hutley. J.	‡Sgt Johnson. D.	Landed on LZ.

Wave Three: Tarrant Rushton 'D' Sqn
(Towed by Halifaxes of 644 & 298 Sqns)
(Allocation known)
Loads:
CN 97–120: 4th A/L Anti-Tank Battery.
CN 121–124: FOO Divisional HQ.
CN 125–126: FOO 3rd Parachute Brigade.

CN.	LZ.	Glider Pilots		Comments
97	N	Maj. Lyne, J. F.	S/Sgt Bridgewater, W.	Landed on LZ
98	N	‡S/Sgt Goodwin, G.	‡Sgt Woodrow, E. W.	Landed on LZ
99	N	†S/Sgt New, R. G.	†Sgt Gibbons, J. R.	Drowned when glider crashed into the sea

100	N	*S/Sgt Dow, A.	†Sgt Chadwick, R.	Landed nr Pont-L'Eveque. Chadwick fatally wounded. Dow captured but later escaped with Shannon and Helme
101	N	Capt. Murdoch, B	Sgt Page, T.	Forced landed 4 miles from Worthy Down. Arrived next day by Hamilcar.
102	N	*Capt. Walker, J. M.	Sgt Carpenter, F.	Landed in River Dives nr Bures. Carpenter badly injured and Walker later captured.
103	N	S/Sgt Higgs, W.	S/Sgt Oliver, W.	Landed on LZ
104	N	‡S/Sgt Rickwood, G. A.	Sgt Gray, J.	Landed on LZ
105	N	S/Sgt Thompson, G.	Sgt Crawley,R.	Landed on LZ
106	N	S/Sgt Browne, G.	Sgt Jones, L	Landed on LZ
107	N	S/Sgt Stevenson, F.	Lt. Moorwood, S. J. D.	Landed on LZ
108	N	‡Lt. Muir, I. C.	Sgt Stones, H.	Landed on LZ
109	N	S/Sgt Smith, A.	Sgt Stephenson, J.	Landed on LZ
110	N	S/Sgt Hunter, J.	Sgt Stonebanks, W.	Hit tree nr Briqueville. Stonebanks killed and Hunter sustained broken leg.
111	N	‡S/Sgt Dodd, W.	Sgt Keeley. J.	Landed on LZ
112	N	‡S/Sgt Statham, W.	Sgt Boswell, L.	Landed on LZ
113	N	‡S/Sgt Bashforth, A.	Sgt Dray, R.	Force landed at Ford.
114	N	S/Sgt Johnson, A.	Sgt D'Eath, J.	Landed nr railway area of Goustranville..
115	N	‡S/Sgt White, R.	Sgt Eason, F.	Landed on LZ
116	N	*S/Sgt Helme, E. B. M.	Sgt Hornsby, N.	Landed at Dozule approx. 10 miles from LZ.
117	N	S/Sgt Coombes, A.	Sgt Usher, R.	Landed on LZ.
118	N	S/Sgt Downing, R.	Sgt Elliott, D.	Landed on LZ.
119	N	*S/Sgt Musitano, P.	†Sgt Perry, S.	Landed half a mile short of LZ.

120	N	S/Sgt Joliffe, R.	Sgt Prentice, A.	Landed on LZ.
121	N	S/Sgt Stocker, E.	Sgt Allen, S.	Landed on LZ.
122	N	S/Sgt England, E.	Sgt Plant, J.	Landed on LZ.
123	N	†S/Sgt Howe, W.	†Sgt Shannon, W.	Came down in sea of Cabourg.
124	N	†S/Sgt Davies, V.	Sgt Cavalli, L.	Landed on LZ.
125	N	†S/Sgt Phillpott, G.	†Sgt Taylor, E.	Glider took direct hit from flak.
126	N	S/Sgt Mackenzie, J.	Sgt Argyll, M.	Landed on LZ

Hamilcars from Tarrant Rushton 'C' Sqn
(Towed by Halifaxes of 644 & 298 Sqns)
(Allocations known)
Loads CN 500–503: 17 Pdr and towing vehicle of 3rd Anti-tank Bty.

CN.	LZ.	Glider Pilots		Comments
500	N	2/Lt.Taylorson, T. W.	Sgt Simpson, R.	Landed on LZ.
501	N	†S/Sgt Ridings, L.	*Sgt Harris, R.	Landed in orchard nr St Vaast en Auge.
502	N	S/Sgt Dent, H.	Sgt Rodgers, D.	Tow-rope broke over Bognor. Landed at Ford.
503	N	S/Sgt England, E.	Sgt Hill, J.	Landed on LZ.

Appendix Two

Killed in Action on Tonga

Name	Rank	Age	Sqn	Place Buried/Commemorated
Beveridge, Henry	Sgt	25	B	Ranville 1A.C.1
Brabham, John Pascal	S/Sgt	23	B	St Desir 6.B.14
Bromley, John Lee	Lt	25	A	Ranville 4A.G.20
Chadwick, Ronald	Sgt	31	D	St Desir 3.A.2
Foster, Peter	Sgt	23	F	La Deliverande 9.A.6
Fuell, John Henry	Sgt	24	E	St Desir 3.A.7
Gibbons, John Robert Maurice	Sgt	27	D	Bayeux Memorial Panel 18 Column 1
Haines, Victor	Sgt	25	A	Abbeville 6.K.1
Hopgood, Colin Harold	S/Sgt	26	B	St Vaast-en-Auge 11
Howe, William Richard	S/Sgt	28	D	Ranville 2A.J.5
Lightowler, Eric	Sgt	24	B	Ranville 5A.E.6
Luff, Roy Samuel	S/Sgt	23	A	Ranville 4A.M.20
Marfleet, William Kenneth	S/Sgt	24	A	Bayeux 10.J.17
Nash, James Harry	Sgt	24	B	Ranville Grave 44
New, Ronald George	S/Sgt	30	D	Ste Marie Le Havre 67.H.15
Ockwell, Herbert Victor	S/Sgt	27	A	Ste Marie Le Havre 67
Perry, Stanley Wood	Sgt	22	D	Ranville 5A.H.4
Phillips, Daniel Francis	Sgt	27	B	St Vaast-en-Auge 8

Phillpott, George Edward	S/Sgt	28	D	Bayeux Memorial Panel 18 Column 1
Powell, Barry	Sgt	22	A	Ranville 4A.J.20
Ridings, Leslie	S/Sgt	23	C	St Vaast-en-Auge 5
Rigg, Alex	Sgt	27	A	Ranville Grave 3
Saunders, Victor Charles	S/Sgt	28	E	St Desir 3.A.6
Stear, Alan Trevor	S/Sgt	23	A	Ranville Grave 10
Stonebanks, William Henry	Sgt	29	D	Brucourt Grave 4
Taylor, Eric Manley	Sgt	25	A	Bayeux Memorial Panel 18 Column 1
Wright, Duncan Frank	S/Sgt	25	A	Ranville 3A.B.2

Bibliography

Published Sources

Ambrose, S. E.: *Pegasus Bridge 6 June 1944*. George Allen & Unwin, 1984.
Belfield, E. & Essame, H.: *The Battle for Normandy*. Purnell Book Services Ltd., 1965.
Chatlerton, G. *The Wings of Pegasus*. Macdonald & Co.
Crookenden, N.: *Dropzone Normandy*. Purnell Book Services Ltd., 1976.
The Eagle—The Regimental Magazine of the Glider Pilot Regiment.—Summer 1954; Summer 1956; April 1986; July 1986; August 1987; April 1988; August 1988; December 1988; April 1989; August 1989; December 1989; August 1990; April 1991; August 1991; December 1991; April 1992.
Golley, J.: *The Big Drop*. Jane's Publishing Company Ltd., 1982.
Hogg. I. V. (Editor): *German Order of Battle 1944*. Purnell Book Services Ltd., 1975.
Hunt, R. & Mason, D.: *The Normandy Campaign*. Purnell Book Services Ltd., 1976.
Jefferson, A.: *Assault on the Guns of Merville*. John Murray, 1987.
Johnson, G. & Dunphie, C.: *Brightly Shone the Dawn*. Frederick Warne (Publishers) Ltd., 1980.
Macksey, K. & Batchelor, J. H.: *Tank*. Macdonald, 1970.
Otway. T. B. H.: *The Second World War 1939–45—Airborne Forces*. Imperial War Museum, 1990.
Saunders, H. St G.: *The Red Beret*. Michael Joseph Ltd., 1953.
Seth, R.: *Lion With Blue Wings*. Victor Gollancz Ltd., 1955.
Smith, C.: *The Glider Pilot Regiment—the Official History*. Pen & Sword Books, 1992.
Weeks, J.: *Assault from the Sky*. Westbridge Books, 1978.
Wilmot, C.: *The Struggle For Europe*. Fontana, 1959.
Wood, A.: *History of the World's Glider Forces*. Patrick Stephens Ltd., 1990.

Unpublished Sources

3 Para Sdn RE War Diary, WO171/151O 145046.
'B' Sdn, GPR War Diary, (Courtesy Major T. I. J. Toler).
8 Para Bn War Diary, (extracts courtesy of Tony Leake).
4 Airlanding Anti-Tank Bty, RA. War Diary—June 1944.
Allocation of Airfields, DZs & LZs, WO171/425.
Enquiries into Missing Personnel, 1939-45 War. North West Europe: gliders and aircraft; 1 Wing, Glider Pilot Regiment, Army Air Corps, WO361/504.

Enquiries into Missing Personnel, 1939-45 War. North West Europe: gliders and aircraft; 2 Wing, Glider Pilot Regiment, Army Air Corps, WO361/505.
Major John Howard's Report 6.6.44., W0171/1387.
S.HQ. Diary, Blakehill Farm, (Courtesy of Edna Morris).
Handwritten debriefing notes for 233 Sqn. RAF from Blakehill Farm
OGP Crew List No. 1 No. 1 Wing, W0171/1230.
OGP Crew List No. 1 No. 2 Wing, W0171/1230.
De-Brief Reports, Op. Overlord.
Glider Raid Reports, AIR27/1647, 186807
Glider Raid Reports, AIR27/1650, 186876
Glider Raid Reports, AIR27/2161, 186876
Pilots' Logs—F. H. Cooil, 295 Sqn RAF; S/Sgt H. N. Andrews & Sgt. W. A. Shannon, GPR.
Written or taped stories from the following—H. N. Andrews, R. Ashby, D. Bailey, G. Barkway, R. Bartley, J. Bowen. F. Corry, C. Dodwell, A. Dow, D. Edwards, R. Falkingham, R. Fellows, R. Hellyer, B. Helme, L. Herbe. H. Humberstone. K. Kirkham, A.
Leake, G. Lockwood, R. Marie, W. Meiklejohn, W. Musitano. G. Nye, F. Ockenden, T. B. H Otway. A. Pickwoad, H. Pond, J. Potts, T. Roseveare, P. Senier, J. Shave, W. Shannon, R. J. Simpson. E. Stocker, G. Tabary, J. Vallois, L. Weeden, E. Wilson, P. Wilson, D. Wood.

Index